WILDERNESS WISDOM

A Sacred Guide to Healing
for the Woman Who Feels Lost

KRIS CALA

THE WILDERNESS
COMPASS

Disclaimer

This book is intended to encourage, educate, and inspire. It does not replace professional medical, legal, financial, or therapeutic advice. Results will vary for each individual, and the author makes no guarantees regarding outcomes. Some names, dates, and locations may have been changed to protect the privacy of individuals.

ISBN: 979-8-9923320-0-1

DEDICATION

To Mom,
For showing me the true meaning of resilience and unconditional love.

To my incredible children,
My greatest blessings and a constant reminder of God's goodness. Watching you grow into strong, kind, and courageous humans is my greatest joy.

Above all, to the Lord,
My True North. Thank You for guiding me through the wilderness with grace, love, and purpose. When You whispered *The Wilderness Compass* into my heart in 2018, I never imagined the journey ahead or how You would use it to lead others through their own wilderness.

TABLE OF CONTENTS

FOREWORD

BY ELIZABETH ENRIGHT PHILLIPS

When I first met Kris, I knew God had a special plan for her. She was vibrant, funny, professional, and accomplished, but I had no idea just how much she would be tested. As her business coach, I had the honor of walking alongside her during one of the most difficult seasons of her life. Real estate investment was our focus, but behind every deal and decision was a storm that could have easily overwhelmed her emotionally, mentally, and financially.

Step by step, the wilderness season intensified. There were days when the weight of it all felt impossible. But Kris held onto Jesus for dear life. In these pages and through her stories, her honesty, and her wisdom, you will find not just a guide but a companion for your own journey through the wilderness. And always, she will point you toward the True North on our compass to guide us through the storms: Jesus Christ.

Maybe you're wondering where God is in all of this. Maybe you're not even sure what you believe anymore. I understand, I truly do. I grew up as the child of two violent divorces, and I know firsthand the deep, lasting impact of that kind of trauma. But I also know something even greater. Healing beyond the wilderness is real. Even when you can't see the way forward, even when you can't imagine ever feeling whole again, I promise you...there is hope.

The transformation I've seen in Kris is nothing short of a miracle. And let me be clear, her healing didn't come overnight or without struggle. She fought for it. She wrestled through uncertainty, setbacks, and moments where the next step wasn't clear. But she kept going. She found her way through, and she came out on the other side stronger, healthier, and more grounded in who she is and what she was called to do. And that's why I know, without a doubt, that healing is real and possible for **you** too.

So, I encourage you, read this book in whatever way you need to. Read it all in one sitting and just take it in. Or go little by little, hide it under your pillow, journal through it, talk it out with a trusted friend. Connect with Kris through her events and coaching. Let this book be a tool to help you take that next small step forward. Because no matter how lost you feel right now, you don't have to stay there.

There is hope.

And no matter where you are in your journey, Kris will always point you back to the One who never stops guiding: Jesus Christ.

Lovingly,

Elizabeth Enright Phillips

Author & REI Coach

ACKNOWLEDGMENTS

Wilderness Wisdom was never meant to be written alone, and it wasn't.

To the women who said yes to sharing their wilderness with me: thank you. Your honesty, vulnerability, and strength brought light to these pages.

Contributing Authors

The following women graciously contributed written chapters that expanded the wisdom in these pages:

- Elizabeth Enright Phillips - *Foreword*
- Cassandra Lennox
- EstherSue Murray
- Michelle Griffin
- Sonja Revells

Featured Interviewees

The following women shared their personal stories through interviews that have been thoughtfully adapted for this book. Their experiences added depth, relatability, and hope:

- Amanda Todd
- Dawn Marie Shroba
- Elizabeth Feldhaus
- Layla Grace Rule
- Linda Violette
- Monica Ann Lewin

- Reina Alicia Kluender

- Suzanne Burns

To my tribe - family, friends, and community, thank you for holding me up through the hardest parts of my wilderness and for reminding me, again and again, that healing happens together. Cassie, thank you for being an amazing writing coach amid sharing your own story.

And to every reader holding this book in your hands: you are part of this story now, too.

We are never meant to walk through the wilderness alone.

INTRODUCTION

This isn't the story I planned. But it is the one that changed everything. It became a defining moment, one that shaped who I am now. But when it was happening, it certainly didn't feel that way.

I most certainly never imagined I'd be telling this story to you, or anyone else.

Not because it's too painful, but because for so long, I didn't think it mattered. I thought people only cared about the other side of it, not the messy middle of it.

I thought I was the only one crawling through the wilderness, unsure if I'd ever feel whole again.

But the more women I meet, the more I hear the same confession:
"I can't believe I'm even here sharing this..."

And every time, I want to reach for their hand and say,

"You're not alone. I've been there too."

This book was born from that moment.

That sacred space where pain meets purpose.

Because here's what I've learned:

Some of the strongest women I know found their purpose in the pit.

Not after it. Not in spite of it. *In it.*

This is not a story of survival.

This is a story of *becoming.*

Of finding faith and strength when life gets wild - and learning to rise anyway.

On my 50th birthday, instead of blowing out candles on a cake, I was dismantling my life. What should have been a milestone celebration filled with fun, family, and friends found me standing isolated, empty, and fully broken on the steps of the Meadowlands Convention Center in New Jersey. There were no candles for me to blow out and when the people in my life called to wish me a happy birthday, I let most of them go to voicemail. I didn't feel like I had anything to celebrate. It took every ounce of energy I had left to be there to watch my oldest daughter compete on the main stage at a dance competition she had always dreamed of. I was so happy for her, yet my heart was unbearably heavy. To be honest, I was a hot mess. The only Party that day was a Pity Party... and yeah, I showed up early and stayed late.

But I had to keep it together. No one around me knew that my life's belongings were stowed into a moving container, being transported toward an uncertain chapter over 600 miles away. That night would be the last I would spend in the house I once thought would be my "forever home". Now I couldn't wait to leave it behind, haunted by the final memories I experienced within its walls. I got sick to my stomach thinking of every time I had to even walk in or out of it. Moving day was tomorrow. "Just get me through tomorrow, Lord," I prayed silently to myself.

I've never felt more confused, alone or scared. I felt like my life was over. I felt like a failure. I was ashamed, depressed, heartbroken, angry, grief stricken and numb.

Lost. Lost in the Wilderness.

Without a clue of what was to come or how I'd get

through the following days, I had so many questions left unanswered. "Why was this happening to me?" I had fought so hard. I tried so hard to do what was right. To be a good person, follow all the rules. "Was God punishing me?" I was so tired, angry and frankly, I struggled to feel faith and hope on what was supposed to be such a highlight of a day and year for me. I have had faith in God since I was 15 and was always taught that He is not the Author of chaos, confusion, darkness and evil. Yet here I found myself questioning the origin of my pain, because I was feeling so severely wounded. I knew deep down that while God allowed it to occur, that humans have free will and this was not His choice for me. For some reason I still questioned. You may have had times you've felt this way, too. You might feel that way now.

The year prior had started off with so many rights, so many wins and so many positives. Now here I was a year later on the steps of the unknown, blankly staring at the huge flight of concrete steps leading up to the convention center not wanting to walk back down them, knowing that once I left them in the past, I'd be leaving way more than just my daughter's dance competition. I'd be leaving the last of the life I'd known for nearly two decades.

Just less than a year earlier, my husband had asked me for a divorce. Two months later, he asked me to reconcile. Five months after that, I filed for divorce. A month after my 50th birthday, it would be final: Marriage Over. I'll share more about that in the chapters to come.

This book is not about pointing fingers or assigning blame. It's about finding your footing again after everything familiar falls apart. It is about navigating those moments in life that feel like a wilderness...dry, disorienting, and full of questions, and realizing that healing, purpose, and even joy can still grow there.

While I do share parts of my story that involve betrayal, heartbreak, and hard truths, I've done so carefully and intentionally. I've chosen not to name names or include identifying details out of respect for privacy. This isn't a tell-all, it's a tell-through. My goal is not to expose anyone, but to offer hope to someone. Maybe that someone is you.

But for now, I want to ask you: have you ever felt utterly lost? Like *really* lost. The feeling of being so lost where nothing makes sense anymore? Where the life you thought you had, the plans you'd made, and the person you believed yourself to be has suddenly vanished, leaving you standing in a void? That version of lost is ugly, lonely and constantly painful, yet numb- all wrapped up in one. It causes you to see things around you through a different lens which causes a filtered distortion of the reality you've always known.

It's not just confusion or uncertainty; it's an aching emptiness. Like the ground beneath you has crumbled, and no matter which way you turn, there's nothing solid to grab onto, and the earth below you seems to fall away in every direction you move, leaving you suspended in this new reality of unfamiliarity. The people and places that once felt safe seem impossibly far away or foreign, and you're left questioning everything: "Who am I? How did I get here? What the heck am I supposed to do now?"

Maybe you've faced moments where the weight of the unknown was so heavy, it felt like you could not even take the next step. Maybe you're frozen in the wilderness, unsure of which way to go, or wondering if there even *is* a way forward. Paralyzed with fear, if you take any step, it will propel you even further into a deeper chasm of chaos that you're already experiencing.

Most of us have faced or may currently be facing a wilderness season: times when everything we thought we knew is shaken to its core. In these moments, it is easy to feel like no one else could possibly understand what we're going through or how we'll ever make it out.

What's worse is the creeping doubt that no one even cares. Or worse yet, that God doesn't see or hear you during these times. Pain and despair whisper lies, convincing you that no one could ever help you through "*this,*" because "*this*" is too hard, too ugly, too messy, and too far gone for anyone to want to dive into.

Sweet friend, here's what I want you to know: **you are not alone**. There is an enemy who would love for you to believe that lie. To stay stuck in the wilderness, to feel hopeless and unseen. But the wilderness isn't just a place of pain; it's a place of transformation. A place where you can find a new level of strength, resilience, trust, knowledge, faith and yes, *even healing. This book is for YOU.*

In the chapters ahead, we'll uncover the tools, truths, and hope that can guide you through the darkest of seasons and into a future that's clearer, stronger, and full of purpose.

As we embark on this journey, we will use a clear framework, what I call the COMPASS, to guide our way forward. This COMPASS Framework stands for Community, Openness, Mindset, Purposeful Movement, Accountability, Support, and Self-Care. Each element offers practical guidance to help you navigate wilderness seasons with clarity and purpose.

Before we dive deeper, I want you to know that a few sections in this book include mentions of sensitive subjects that may be triggering. Your emotional safety matters greatly. Prior to each of these sections, I'll gently alert you with a "yield symbol" ∇ and clearly indicate the page number you can turn to if you'd prefer to skip that section. Please honor your feelings and boundaries, choosing what's best for you at each step. You might consider returning to these sections at a later time if you're reading in a place where you can safely allow your feelings to flow unhindered.

Along our path, you'll also find reflection points and journaling prompts. These moments are designed intentionally, giving you space to pause, dig deep, and gain insights specific to your own wilderness journey. Consider them to be steppingstones guiding you gently toward healing and transformation.

Recently, after a hurricane hit our area, my oldest daughter and I walked to the beach to survey the damage. The wind nearly knocked us down, and the waves roared with power. The ocean reminded me of life, how its beauty and destruction can coexist. Constant slow erosion over time slowly causes an ultimate caving in of a larger structure causing devastating damage that leaves the original structure often unrecognizable but sometimes even more beautiful and unique than before. In the same way, our wilderness seasons may feel overwhelming, but they can also shape us, revealing God's presence and direction in unexpected ways.

This book is for anyone stuck in their wilderness or coming out of it and not knowing where to go next. For the one who feels lost, uncertain, broken or afraid. For the one who desperately needs to find the compass to point them towards their next step. I've been there - on the mountaintop one moment, only to be flattened by the desert winds the next. The wilderness can feel endless, like you're wandering in circles. But even there, God shows up, offering guidance, provision, and hope, often in ways we don't recognize at the time.

In these pages, we'll journey through the wilderness together - those raw, uncertain seasons of life that shape us in unexpected ways. When I first began to share my own story, I was met by a chorus of women who quietly raised their hands and said, "Me too." Their courage to speak up reminded me that none of us are truly alone in this.

Throughout this book, I'll offer lessons I've learned and introduce the voices of other brave Wilderness Warriors who have walked through loss, change, and challenges. Some of these women have shared their stories through interviews that appear at the end of chapters, while others have authored entire chapters themselves, bringing their unique wisdom to the page.

This book is not here to convince you of anything - but it is an honest and heartfelt testimony of how I've seen God's hand and felt His presence in the hardest parts of my life. As you read, I invite you to remain open - to your own truth, to the insights of others, and to whatever source of strength helps you find your way forward.

We also explore practical, actionable tips that can be applied without faith or a connection to divinity. However, I want to acknowledge that many of these insights were born from my own journey of faith and connection to my Lord and Savior, Jesus Christ. He has shown me such grace, mercy, love and provision during these times. My goal is to offer hope, direction, and guidance to anyone facing challenging times, in ways that resonate and inspire action, regardless of their beliefs.

While my faith is at the heart of what grounds and guides me, I've also done a lot of inner work over the years - through counseling, research, and personal growth practices that have helped me heal and grow. During that time, I was introduced to powerful therapeutic approaches like Inner Child Work, Trauma-Focused Cognitive Behavioral Therapy (TF-CBT), EMDR, Imagery Rescripting, and Internal Family Systems (IFS). These modalities played an important role in my personal journey, and while I'm not a licensed therapist, they have influenced how I support others as a coach.

Therapists play a vital role in helping us heal from the past, process trauma, and navigate mental and emotional health. As a Life and Business Coach, my work complements that process by helping women take their next steps forward, whether they are currently in therapy, transitioning out of it, or simply ready for what comes next.

I support women through life's wilderness seasons, including separation and divorce, burnout, career shifts, identity crises, and other major life transitions. My role is to help them clarify their goals, shift unhelpful mindsets, build sustainable habits, and stay accountable to the healing and growth they desire.

In addition to personal coaching, I also work with organizations and teams to create strategic solutions around leadership development, workplace wellness, and team performance. Whether guiding individuals or leading groups, my focus is always the same: to ask powerful questions, offer fresh perspective, and equip people with the tools they need to move forward with clarity and purpose.

I have always been a lifelong learner and a natural encourager, someone who sees the best in people and believes in their ability to rise, even from the hardest places. My background in psychology and professional development has shaped my approach, blending optimism with tools that inspire action and meaningful growth.

For over 20 years, my heart has been most full while I have worked to support and walk alongside women during life's wilderness seasons. My experience includes serving as a crisis worker for a domestic violence shelter, a case manager for a therapy program for women and children impacted by abuse and serving on boards and leadership for nonprofits serving teen or single mothers. I have also led bible-based support groups for women healing from trauma and navigating life transitions such as separation and divorce.

If you do not currently have a relationship with God, I invite you to approach the stories and examples I share with an open mind. These reflections are meant to help you consider whether you feel led to open, or reopen, the door to a connection with the Creator.

The goal is to help you and all of us through these seasons so that we don't stay stuck in them for so long that they become more than they are supposed to. In the book of Exodus, after being enslaved by the Egyptians for 430 years, God rescued and delivered the Israelites out of the hands of their captors in one night. However, they wandered for forty years in the wilderness before arriving at the promised land because they were afraid of what waited in the unknown. They forgot the miracles performed and the promises God made to them about His protection and what He told them about the promised land.

We do not want to be stuck in the wilderness any longer than we need to be. We do not want to lose sight of what the promised land holds, it must be our guiding light. If we lose sight of it, we wander off the path. If we lack a Compass, we lack direction.

Just as our fingerprints are unique, so too are the paths God uses to lead us to His promises.

Let's explore the Wilderness together, because once you shine a light on something it no longer can stay hidden in the darkness.

My hope is that the lessons in this book will become your compass, pointing you toward clarity, hope, and the best life God has for you. Let's take the first step together. We've got this.

PART 1:
UNDERSTANDING
THE WILDERNESS

1
WHAT IS THE WILDERNESS?

"See, I am doing a new thing!
Now it springs up; do you not perceive it?
I am making a way in the wilderness
and streams in the wasteland."
— Isaiah 43:19 (NIV)

Regardless of how you find yourself in the wilderness, it's often triggered by something unexpected: a traumatic event, a major disruption to your routine, the loss of a loved one, a sudden illness, a career upheaval, estrangement, or an earth-shattering revelation.

For me, it was the moment my husband asked for a divorce, unraveling the life I had spent years building. Sometimes, it's something harder to name, like an ache, a shift, or a quiet emptiness that doesn't fit neatly into a category. But whatever it is, your wilderness is personal. And it is real.

When that "big thing" happens, it feels like your entire world stops. Time slows, yet life keeps moving on without you. You find yourself wandering in uncharted territory, asking: *"How did I get here?"* and *"How do I find my way out?"*

The wilderness is disorienting. One moment, you are feeling lost and fumbling in the dark, trying to figure out where you are. The next, it feels like the walls are closing in, trapping you in a rapid intensity. You crouch in fear, bracing for the next impact, only to find yourself wandering again, flashlight in hand, trying to make sense of it all as you navigate the wide-open expanse of unknown.

For me, my wilderness season began just under a year before my 50th birthday. That birthday marked the end of one chapter of my wilderness season and the beginning of another - one I never wanted to write. Everything happened so fast yet felt agonizingly slow at the same time.

It started on November 3, 2021, when I became sick with COVID. I had thought I'd dodged the virus after over a year and a half of avoiding it, but it certainly showed up in full force.

I thought the virus alone would be enough to derail me. It wasn't.

During my 13 days of isolation, I was sicker than I had ever been. My fever climbed to 103.5, I had a splitting headache, body aches that left me in such pain and so weak, and I struggled with every other symptom of COVID except the loss of taste. I barely had the strength to get out of bed, and I felt incredibly alone. This was still the time when recommendations were to be fully isolated from others, so I was tucked away neatly into my home's guest bedroom.

My husband made sure food was delivered to me and checked in from time to time, but the emotional distance between us felt like a void I couldn't cross. The man who once promised to love me in sickness and in health now felt like a stranger. I sensed something was off in the pit of my stomach, and I just couldn't shake it. I kept wondering if I was so sick that my sense of perception was skewed. Was I hallucinating? In the past, during any illness, recovery, or health scare, his behavior had always been different. Thirteen days is a long time. By the end of it, I could not take it anymore. I finally came to and realized something was really, *really* off.

It was like those invisible heat waves that trigger smoke alarms even when you can't see or smell smoke. You just *feel* the fire. That's what I was experiencing.

When I confronted him about his coldness, he exploded. He deflected with anger and suddenly started complaining about the state of our marriage. I stared at him blankly and thought, *"Say what now?"* Then he left. My husband never left. He *always* slept at home. I was absolutely dumbfounded. I couldn't understand what was happening. My state of mind, already fragile and foggy, began to spin. It felt like I was back at day one of being sick.

Let me explain a little about who I am, just to give this some context. I am an Italian girl born and raised in New Jersey. I have worked hard to overcome what sometimes feels like kryptonite running in my veins—the need to hold everything together, especially in the face of someone else's wrongdoing. When someone close to me hurts me, or worse, hurts someone else, the righteous anger in me kicks in and my mouth tends to rise to meet my body temperature. So, you can probably imagine where my head and mouth were at that point.

The very next day, he asked for a divorce.

My world was crumbling. Two daughters living in our home with us, unaware of the storm brewing. My son, thousands of miles away, serving in the military, removed from what was happening at home. Two businesses, our home, church friends & neighborhood & community, our entire life together falling apart before my eyes.

I begged him for answers, but initially, he denied everything, including the affair. Making me question my own sanity, as I often did over the years about several things. But only two months earlier, we had been in Key West on a second honeymoon, celebrating 18 years of marriage and working to reconnect and strengthen things. For months leading up to that there had been stress and strain, due to pressure from running our businesses. But that was normal at this point in our relationship. A long-lasting cycle that continued to repeat. How could everything change so quickly?

It was not until about a month later that my husband confessed his infidelity which he claimed had begun shortly before I became ill with COVID. But in my heart, I knew it had been building for much longer. I had sensed an emotional distance between us for quite some time leading up to that moment, and hearing his admission only confirmed what I had already suspected. The betrayal was compounded by the fact that it involved someone I trusted, making the pain even more profound. Our marriage had already weathered its share of challenges, but this revelation broke something in me and left me questioning everything about my life.

Have you ever felt like your life was circling the drain? That was my wilderness. It was not just about what happened, it was about everything that came after. The confusion, the disorientation, the sense that I had lost myself completely. I could not recognize the woman in the mirror.

Wilderness seasons don't always look the same on the outside, but inside, they often carry the same weight, feeling lost, invisible, stuck, or unsure how to move forward. Mine just happened to start with a divorce. Yours may look entirely different, but the ache? That is where we meet.

The wilderness is more than a physical space, it is a state of being where everything you thought you knew is called into question. In the Bible, the wilderness is often depicted as a place of wandering, testing, and transformation. The Israelites circled the same ground for 40 years, tempted and distracted, struggling to trust God's promises. They often ignored His constant warnings and directions. Did you know the Bible mentions the wilderness approximately 300 times? It is a recurring theme of challenge and growth.

Take a moment to think about your own wilderness.

Where did it begin?

What did it take from you? What has it revealed?

You don't need to have it all figured out. You just need to be willing to name it, even if only in a whisper.

In our modern life, the wilderness can look like:

- **Being stuck**: Feeling like you're going in circles, unable to move forward. This can show up in many ways, one being ruminating thoughts or patterns. Sometimes people will say things like, "The definition of insanity is doing the same thing over and over, expecting different results." This can be hurtful and demeaning to someone who genuinely wants change but doesn't know how to begin because they are overwhelmed by something that seems too big.

- **Being tempted**: Distracted by shiny paths or quick fixes that pull you away from real healing. For example, moving from one relationship into another without taking the time to heal.

- **Being lost**: Searching for direction, unsure of where your true north is or how to get back on track. When we wander, it can be really confusing and disorienting.

Yet, the wilderness is not just a place of pain, it's breathtakingly beautiful in its own way.

Yes, I can say that now.

It's raw, wild, and untamed. It's a place of adventure and awe, even in its messiness. It forces you to face the reality of who you are, where you've been, and who you're becoming. This can be really uncomfortable, and I understand this is why so many people avoid dealing directly with their wilderness seasons. Or why so many people get stuck ruminating on what brought them there and are not able to move forward after the season ends. It's also important to note that the wilderness is not a place of punishment or God's way of inflicting wrath on you. Many people often mistake trials and tribulations as damnation. God is clear in His Word that He is not the source of sin, evil or pain. However, He does promise that when you go THROUGH trials and tribulations and that He will be WITH you to GUIDE you to the other side of them.

"When you pass through the waters, I will be with you; and through the rivers, they shall not overflow you. When you walk through the fire, you shall not be burned, nor shall the flame scorch you." Isaiah 43:2

"My brethren, count it all joy when you fall into various trials, knowing that the testing of your faith produces patience. But let patience have its perfect work, that you may be perfect and complete, lacking nothing." James 1:2-4

The wilderness has a purpose. It's a time of testing, training, and preparation. In my experience, God is not absent in the wilderness, He is walking beside you, leading you toward transformation that yields both great growth, miracles and yes, even joy. If you're feeling stuck in the wilderness, begin by asking yourself:

- What brought me here? Was it a specific event, choice, or unexpected change?

- Am I wandering in circles? Are there patterns in my life that keep repeating?

- What distractions are keeping me stuck? Have I followed paths that seemed appealing but didn't lead to healing?

- Am I ignoring dealing with my pain or issues and running to the next thing instead of working on what it takes to become the healthiest version of myself?

The wilderness isn't the end of your story, it's the beginning of your transformation. In the next chapter, we'll explore the "big thing" that brings us to the wilderness and how to confront it with honesty and courage.

2
WHAT LANDED US HERE?

"Some changes look negative on the surface, but you will soon realize that space is being created in your life for something new to emerge."
-Eckhart Tolle

It's hard to imagine that anything good could emerge from devastation, but that's the nature of the wilderness. Often it begins with a single moment, a turning point, one we don't see coming and sometimes don't realize until later that it was the thing that moved everything off course.

At the start of my separation, I was riding one of the biggest career highs of my life. About 8 years earlier, I had left a successful career in real estate sales that spanned a decade before joining a national corporation to work as a business development executive in higher education and healthcare, working to provide strategic workforce solutions to large businesses and their teams. I made the move due to my husband and I launching family businesses, so he could operate them while my "more stable" corporate job gave us the steady, dependable income and benefits while getting the family businesses off the ground.

In the year before my separation and at the start of the pandemic, I returned to real estate as an agent and began flipping properties as a real estate investor, while still working my full-time job. Over that year, I made multiple large income gains in a very short time. This finally gave me the ability to do what I had always wanted to, and I left my near decade long W2 career in the corporate workplace to return to real estate and continue investing full-time. I was excited to be back in real estate and investing because now I was applying skills from what I'd learned from my experience and the additional education (I had recently completed my master's degree) over my career which equipped me in a new way. From the outside, it looked like everything was falling into place, like I had it all together - a thriving career and a stable family life. But behind the scenes, my marriage was unraveling.

Nearly a year after the betrayal happened, I woke up on my 50th birthday, less than a month before the divorce finalizing, feeling completely lost and heartbroken. I felt unprepared for life as a single mother. I chose to start over somewhere new; to be closer to my support system several states away from where my husband and I had built our life and careers together. My marriage ending had brought me so much shame, guilt, embarrassment and depression. In an instant, everything I had built- my marriage, my family, careers, and the future I thought was secure, was gone. I felt like such a failure. I worked so hard to keep everything looking like nothing was wrong, covering up any imperfections or flaws our life may have shown, both publicly and privately. I was spinning all the plates myself. Once one fell, the rest followed suit.

What I thought would be the best year of my life became the most awful to date. Witnessing my children's revelation of the truth about what was going on was one of the most difficult things I've ever experienced. It hurt as much as finding out the truth myself. I instantly felt like the veil was lifted off of their heads and they could clearly see the world's ugliest truths and now had to deal with them head on. I can imagine how painful that was for them. This made me feel even worse.

As I mentioned earlier, right before I became ill with COVID, my husband began an affair- though I wouldn't learn that truth until weeks later. He later admitted to the timing, but deep down, I felt it had been emotionally building long before. I had sensed in my spirit something - I remember going to sleep every night for almost 2 years before this happened with the nagging feeling inside that I was sleeping next to a stranger, a man I no longer knew. I always felt so odd about that and couldn't shake it. But nothing could have prepared me for the magnitude of what was to come. The betrayal was even more painful because it involved someone I trusted, compounding my heartbreak and disillusionment.

I keep coming back to one moment that marked the end of so much: sitting in the audience at my daughter's dance competition, knowing it would be the last day in the home I had poured my heart into - the home I once believed was forever. I was so proud of her, but my heart was shattered. It wasn't just the end of a marriage - it was the unraveling of my identity, my sense of security, and the life I thought I had built. I loved that home, but I knew I couldn't stay. For so many reasons, it was time to let it go.

I even had to get rid of my chickens and the huge garden I'd cultivated during the pandemic. I loved those chickens, darn it. Those were my COVID chickens. Cute, fluffy butt chickens that made me so happy every time I walked out my back door. Stupid, clueless chickens that ate all the elderberries off my tree and made my daughter so happy because she loved them so much. I also had agreed for my 2 dogs to go with my husband, which hurt way more than the chickens. But I knew I couldn't take them where I was going. My daughters had to deal with the reality that they were leaving their father and moving so far away. They were heartbroken. Everything that was once wonderful now sucked.

I had spent decades defining myself as a wife, mother, professional and entrepreneur, and suddenly, all of that crumbled. I was starting over from scratch, untangling the complex strands of a life built on shared businesses, finances, property, and even my name. I thought my life was over at 50 years old. I felt completely out of my element.

I spiraled into unhealthy coping mechanisms. I drank to numb the pain, ate whatever was easy, causing me to sink into isolation and gain a ton of weight. I didn't want to talk to anyone. I wasn't in the mood for advice or encouragement, and I certainly didn't want to go out and meet new people.

Honestly, I was pissed off.

Bitter. I felt like a fool.

And I was MAD.

Mad that I had tried to do all the right things for people, only to be taken advantage of.

Mad that I had believed my good intentions and deeds would somehow earn me a perfect life.

I was completely off-kilter - emotionally, spiritually, and mentally unanchored.

My victim mindset was in full force.

The night after Christmas in 2022, I hit rock bottom. I

drank enough wine to try to forget about everything. My daughters were gone for two weeks visiting their father. It was the longest I had ever been without them. I felt completely out of control, knowing they were hurting, and that the version of their dad they were spending time with was confusing and painful for them. There was nothing I could do to shield them from the truth, or from the heartache of seeing him in the state he was in. He wasn't coping well either, he had grown deeply depressed and negative about everything.

The next morning, I woke up ashamed and humiliated, staring down at the reality of what my life had become. I knew I couldn't keep spiraling like this. If I didn't make a change, things were going to get much worse.

This was my wilderness moment: a place of heartbreak, loss, and deep uncertainty. I had to confront the harsh truth: if I didn't change, I would risk losing even more. My kids, my health, my finances...everything was at stake. It was the wake-up call I needed to begin the slow and painful journey toward healing.

The Wilderness Waypoint

Each wilderness season has a waypoint I refer to as the "big thing." It's the moment that shakes you up - your personal mile marker. It might be an "aha" moment, a turning point, or the realization that you're stuck in fear, heartbreak, or uncertainty, and something really needs to change.

For me, it was allowing my divorce to define me. I functioned as though my life had ended simply because my marriage had failed. I couldn't heal or move forward until I faced the truth: I was betraying myself by staying stuck in something I knew was causing more harm than good. I had to take action and begin doing what was best for me.

Your "big thing" might look different. It could be a job loss, the death of a loved one, a health crisis, or a major life change. Neglect, betrayal, abuse, addiction, injury, grief, separation or divorce, estrangement, and mental health struggles often become the catalyst that sends us into the wilderness. These seasons usually involve some form of trauma that disrupts the flow of our hearts, minds, and daily lives.

The wilderness is not just a place of loss. It is where we confront our reality and the choices that brought us here. It is messy, confusing, and often heartbreaking. But it is also where transformation begins.

Scripture often uses the wilderness as a metaphor for struggle and refinement. The Israelites wandered for forty years, tested and tempted on their way to the Promised Land. Jesus fasted in the wilderness for forty days before beginning His ministry. These stories mirror our own seasons of testing, times when we face distractions, doubts, and detours.

You may experience more than one wilderness season in your lifetime. Some shape our beliefs and behaviors early on, while others appear later and force us to re-examine how those early experiences are still affecting us. The things that happen to us when we're young often leave marks that follow us well into adulthood.

Maybe your wilderness moment didn't come all at once. Maybe it was a slow unraveling, an ache that built up over time. Maybe you didn't even realize how lost you felt until everything around you began to fall apart.

Whatever your experience, I want you to know this:

You are not weak for being here.

You are not broken beyond repair.

You are standing at the edge of something sacred, a chance to rebuild, redefine, and rise.

Before we go any further:

Breathe.
Reflect.

What has your wilderness moment looked like? What are you afraid to name or feel?

You don't need to fix it right now.

You just need to see it.

Acknowledge it.

Because healing begins with honesty.

As a young teen, I longed for validation and love. I craved the kind of attention I thought would make me feel whole, especially from men. So, when I finally found someone who felt safe, my very first boyfriend, I clung to him like a child clings to a blanket. He came from a healthy family. I did not. I didn't know how to behave in a healthy relationship. I had no model for it. I only knew how to create drama, push people away, then beg for their forgiveness and attention again. I'm deeply remorseful for the way I handled that relationship, but it was all I knew at the time.

Growing up without a consistent, healthy father in my life left me feeling unworthy of good things, especially love. My father struggled with addiction and undiagnosed mental illness. He and my mother divorced when I was 9. He was not a safe or stable presence in my childhood and was often incarcerated due to criminal behavior. When I was with him, I was not cared for properly. As a result, I internalized the belief that I didn't deserve to be protected, valued, or safe with men, especially those closest to me.

That belief system began when I was five years old. A young adult neighbor who babysat me after kindergarten exposed himself and attempted to violate me. I didn't fully understand what was happening at the time. To this day, I don't remember all the details. After many therapy sessions, I've accepted that I may never know everything, and that's okay. What I do know is this: his actions were abusive, and that alone is enough to acknowledge and grieve.

When I told my father what happened, he did nothing. He didn't protect me. He didn't make me feel safe. Looking back, I'm proud of my five-year-old self for even speaking up. Many children can't find the words to do that. But my father dismissed me, and in that moment, I began questioning myself. I doubted my memory and my ability to trust my own truth.

Shortly after that, I found myself left in that neighbor's care again. I remember him laughing and playing with my younger brother, lifting him into the air while I stood in the same room, invisible. As a five-year-old, I didn't know how to process the rejection. I had told the truth, yet I was being punished for it. I remember asking him, "Why aren't you playing with me anymore?" He looked me in the eyes and said, "Because you told your dad about the other day, and now I don't want to play with you anymore."

The next thing I did would shape how I saw my worth in the eyes of men for years to come: I begged him to forgive me. I begged him to play with me again.

Through therapy and deep inner work, I eventually

began to understand how much that moment had shaped me. I carried the belief that protecting myself would lead to abandonment and shame. So, I didn't protect myself. I kept silent when people hurt me. If someone insulted me, I said nothing. If someone lied or cheated, I made excuses. If someone used me, I blamed myself and felt worthless.

One of the books that helped me begin to heal was "No Bad Parts" by Dr. Richard Schwartz, the founder of Internal Family Systems (IFS). The IFS approach teaches us how to acknowledge the different parts of ourselves, especially the ones burdened by trauma, and relate to them with compassion. The goal is to help those parts release the pain they've been carrying so we can return to a sense of wholeness.

One exercise that brought deep healing for me was revisiting that memory from a new perspective. I envisioned my adult self, kneeling beside my five-year-old self and saying:

"I'm so sorry this happened to you. I'm sorry your dad didn't protect you. You did nothing wrong. You deserved love, safety, and care. You are precious and worthy of protection. You never have to beg for someone's attention, especially not someone who devalues your humanity."

Then, I asked my inner child to help me rewrite the ending. In this new version, I screamed "No," kicked the neighbor, and ran into the arms of a father who believed me. A father who protected me. A father who had that man arrested.

I revisit that healing version whenever the old feelings creep back in. It reminds me that I am seen. I am safe. And I am worthy of love and protection.

This practice combines Inner Child work and Imagery

Rescripting, both powerful tools for healing past trauma.

Reflective Prompt:

What past experiences may still be influencing your current choices?

Is there a moment from your childhood you'd like to revisit and rewrite with your younger self?

If so, I encourage you to explore this with the guidance of a licensed counselor or therapist. The wilderness forces us to pause and ask the tough questions such as:

How did I get here?

What needs to change?

What is preventing me from healing?

Identify Your "Big Thing"

Take a moment to reflect on your wilderness season. What was the "big thing" that brought you here? Maybe it was one major event. Maybe it was a thousand little things that slowly unraveled your life. You might even have more than one wilderness experience. Whatever it is, name it.

Ask yourself:

- What brought me here?
- What feelings or beliefs are keeping me stuck?
- What distractions are pulling me off course?

This is the first step toward healing and transformation:

Acknowledging where you are and how you got here.

In the next chapter, we'll explore how to navigate the wilderness and begin the journey toward finding your true north.

As we journey through this first part of the book, reflecting on the origins of our Wilderness Seasons and the paths that land us there, I want to introduce you to a story that speaks directly to the heart, both physical and spiritual.

EstherSue Murray's wilderness journey is one of profound faith, transformation, and surrender. Her experience begins with the unimaginable: discovering that her unborn child would be born with a severe congenital heart defect. But her story is not just about physical trials. It is a testament to the heart-work God performs in us during our darkest seasons.

Her story reminds us that even in the most desolate wilderness, God is present, refining and transforming us for His purpose. It is only fitting as we work to transition through Part 1: Understanding the Wilderness to prepare for Part 2: Navigating the Wilderness with Your COMPASS with this story, as it reflects the foundation of the **COMPASS Framework**: surrender, strength, and faith guiding us through the most challenging times.

3
SPIRITUAL HEART SURGERY

By EstherSue Murray

A voice cries:
"In the wilderness prepare the way of the LORD;
Make straight in the desert a highway for our God."
Isaiah 40:3 ESV

It is in the desert where God shows up. It is in our wilderness seasons that we truly see Him. These seasons, allowed by God, open our hearts and minds to His work—molding, shaping, and transforming us into the beautiful human He designed us to be. Don't miss the deep heart-work God is doing as He transforms you into His masterpiece.

My desert season was long, dry, difficult, uncertain, and scary, as many wilderness seasons are. But mine began with something less common.

I was happily pregnant with my second child. It was a joyous time, knowing that this baby would be just 15 months younger than our son, Justin. At 24 weeks gestation, during a routine sonogram, I was told to follow up with my OBGYN. The staff gave me hugs and said "good luck" as I left. I thought they were being overly friendly, totally oblivious to what they already knew and what I was about to find out.

That evening, my husband and I met with the OBGYN after hours, another sign I missed. The doctor was visibly upset, pacing, running his hands through his hair, and muttering:

"Oh my God!"

"I've never seen this before!"

"We're screwed!"

"This is bad. Really, really bad!"

I was still clueless. My motherly instinct wanted to console him, not realizing the weight of what he was about to tell us. He referred us to another specialist at Manhasset University Hospital in Syosset, NY, an hour from home.

At Manhasset hospital, everything felt normal until the doctor walked in with a pamphlet. My husband noticed it first. Pregnant women aren't usually handed pamphlets during routine visits. That small booklet about congenital heart defects changed everything. Our baby would be born with half of her heart, a condition called tricuspid atresia. The right side of her heart never formed. As the weight of this diagnosis sank in, I realized I had entered the wilderness.

Questions, fears, and anger consumed me. I was furious with God. I screamed at Him:

*"God, You say,

'I praise you, for I am fearfully and wonderfully made.

Wonderful are your works; my soul knows it very well.'

Psalm 139:14

You lie! Your Word isn't true! My baby isn't wonderfully made! My baby is flawed, broken, and might not even live! You've failed me, God! You've failed me, and now I am alone in my hurt, fear, and darkness."*

I woke up every day in this dark place, unable to care for myself or my unborn baby. I was so alone, and the feelings of abandonment consumed me. Deep down, I knew I couldn't do this alone and that only God could help me. That sense of isolation and helplessness brought me to a moment of total surrender.

I cried out to God:

"Help me!"

The same God I was so angry with became my only source of help and relief. I needed strength beyond my own supernatural strength. I needed my own spiritual open-heart surgery to survive the journey that loomed before me. How ironic that the mother carrying a baby who would require three open-heart surgeries needed her own "heart surgery" to get through the days, weeks, and years ahead.

I trusted what I needed to do... total surrender! I gave myself, my baby, and our future to God. Do you know what comes from surrendering fully to our Lord and Savior Jesus Christ? Incomparable inner strength and peace. Visitors would come during my pregnancy and say, "You are so calm and happy. How are you able to be so strong?"

The strength and peace that God's Holy Spirit gave me on the inside became evident on the outside. I began to see how God was using my pain, struggle, and trial for His glory. I realized how strength builds upon strength, and how we are transformed from glory to glory when we truly allow Him to work in us.

"Blessed are those whose strength is in you,

in whose heart are the highways to Zion.

As they go through the Valley of Baca, they make it a place of springs;

the early rain also covers it with pools.

They go from strength to strength;

each one appears before God in Zion."

Psalm 84:5-7 ESV

Jessica Sue Murray was born at 36 weeks gestation on August 7, 1998, weighing 7 lbs., 4 oz. She was the "monster baby" in the PICU among the preemies. She had no right ventricle and four holes in her heart, a challenging scenario for a newborn. Because of the four holes, her red and blue blood mixed, allowing her to get just enough oxygen to survive. She was discharged the next day.

This gave me a profound spiritual analogy: just as Jessica needed oxygen to survive, I needed God's word as my spiritual oxygen to sustain me. Without daily time in His word, I would not have had the strength to face the journey ahead. I began to crave spending time with God. My mom repeatedly told me, "God can heal her." But I lacked the faith to believe it. I dismissed her words until I read about the Dunamis power of the Holy Spirit: the same power that raised Christ from the dead.

"If the Spirit of Him who raised Jesus from the dead dwells in you,

He who raised Christ Jesus from the dead will also give life to your mortal bodies through His Spirit who dwells in you."

Romans 8:11 ESV

The power that raised Jesus from the dead lived in me. If that was true, then yes, God could heal Jessica's heart. What joy comes from surrendering to Jesus!

To stay grounded, I developed a daily structure for prayer using the acronym PRAY:

- P: Praise Him
- R: Repent
- A: Ask
- Y: Yield

This gave me the focus I needed to rely on Him instead of my circumstances.

Jessica underwent three open-heart surgeries before she turned three. **Today, she is 26 years old, one of the first-generation adults with her condition.** Once I surrendered to His plan, the path He had already prepared became not only bearable but conquerable. God stretched me, strengthened me, and drew me closer to Him through every step of that journey. I would never wish to bypass my wilderness season because of who I became on the other side.

"Count it all joy, my brothers, when you meet trials of various kinds, for you know that the testing of your faith produces steadfastness."

—James 1:2-3

God's ways are higher than ours, and His plans are always faithful and sure. If you are in the wilderness, trust Him. He's got you.

"Oh LORD, You are my God;

I will exalt You;

I will praise Your name, for You have done wonderful things,

plans formed of old, faithful and sure."

Isaiah 25:1

4
TEMPTATIONS

"For we do not have a high priest who is unable to sympathize with our weaknesses, but one who in every respect has been tempted as we are, yet without sin."
Hebrews 4:15 (KJV)

Temptation is not always loud or obvious. Sometimes, it shows up in moments of exhaustion, loneliness, or uncertainty. It may take the form of an unhealthy relationship, a destructive habit, or even something that looks like comfort but leads us away from healing. When we are in the wilderness, temptation has a way of disguising itself as relief.

I learned this firsthand. One of the most pivotal moments in my healing journey came when I chose to invest in myself. At the time, I had no idea what I was doing. I asked myself, "How do I rebuild my life when I don't even know what I want anymore?" But I learned that you don't have to have all the answers to begin. You just have to take one step. Clarity often comes through action.

So, I started. I leaned into books, podcasts, therapy, and coaching. I hired life coaches, business coaches, even a style coach. I was desperate to figure out who I was now and what I actually wanted. None of it was easy. But I knew I couldn't do it alone. I needed structure, wisdom, and a plan, and I needed to learn how to resist the pull of old patterns.

It wasn't just about rebuilding my finances. I needed to heal my heart and mind after divorce. I needed to untangle myself from unhealthy relational dynamics and, most importantly, from the lies I had believed about myself. I even made the decision to change my name. That was not a light decision, but it felt deeply personal and necessary.

As I took those steps, I returned to a full-time job to secure my income and began rebuilding routines that prioritized my physical and mental well-being. I started choosing self-care, even when it was uncomfortable. That meant learning to say no, establishing boundaries, and practicing habits that supported my growth. But that didn't mean the temptation to quit disappeared.

I am a recovering perfectionist. If you can relate, send me a virtual high-five. People like us often feel tempted to give up when something is too hard, too messy, or doesn't go exactly as planned. But what I've learned is that **lasting change is often born through disruption**. It requires us to face discomfort and stay in it long enough to build something new.

One of my biggest breakthroughs was accepting that **progress is more important than perfection**. I had to get honest about the way I traded commitment for convenience. And I had to fight through that pattern with intentional tools. One resource that helped me was *Atomic Habits* by James Clear. It taught me how to build change one small, consistent step at a time.

But more than habit hacking, I had to reconnect with my deeper "why."

Temptation often comes when we forget what we are moving toward. When we lose sight of our purpose, we start looking for relief in the wrong places. That is when we are most vulnerable to accepting relationships, jobs, habits, or beliefs that are less than what God wants for us. I have been there, settling for something I knew wasn't right simply because it was easier than waiting or working through the hard stuff.

Sometimes temptation comes packaged as something beautiful. A person, a job, a belief, or a shortcut that promises to solve everything quickly. But it costs us. It chips away at our values and slowly pulls us off course. And often, we don't even see it happening until we feel stuck or distant from the healing we were working toward.

That's why it is so important to stay grounded in truth. Scripture reminds us:

"No temptation has overtaken you that is not common to man. God is faithful, and He will not let you be tempted beyond your ability, but with the temptation He will also provide the way of escape, that you may be able to endure it."
1 Corinthians 10:13

You are not alone in this battle. You are not the only one struggling to make good choices in hard seasons. The enemy would love for you to believe that you are too far gone, too broken, or too inconsistent to change. But that is a lie.

Jesus Himself was tempted in the wilderness. And what did He do? He fought back with the Word of God. He stood on truth. He stayed grounded in His identity. He did not argue or debate with the enemy. He simply declared what was already written.

That is your invitation too.

You do not have to fight temptation in your own strength. You have the Word. You have the Spirit of God living in you. You have promises that cannot be broken. And you have a purpose that is too important to delay.

So, when temptation comes, and it will, remind yourself of who you are. Speak life over your identity. Choose the next right thing. And when you fall, do not stay down. Get back up. God always provides a way of escape.

Reflective Prompts:

- What past experiences may be influencing your current choices?

- What temptations are holding you back from healing?

- What are you seeking in relationships?

- Are there fears or past wounds influencing your decisions?

- How can you address those fears to open yourself to healthy habits and growth?

You are stronger than you think. And you are never fighting alone.

5

WANDERING IN THE WILDERNESS

"Faith must be tested, because it can be turned into a personal possession only through conflict"
Oswald Chambers - My Utmost for His Highest

In the aftermath of my divorce, I felt like I was starting over from scratch. I was untangling the intertwined strands of a union that had so many connections, business, finances, legal, administrative, children, property, assets and even my own name. I thought my life was over at 50. I felt broken and utterly unsure of who I was. I began drinking to numb the incredible pain I was experiencing, especially when my kids were gone. I ate poorly like it was my new full-time job. I had gained weight quickly and lack of physical activity wasn't helping.

I had been a wife and mother for two decades, and now, I didn't know who I was outside of that. It was a very uncomfortable place to be, and I felt isolated and completely out of my element. I remember waking up on the day after Christmas in 2022 not remembering anything about the night before. I was so depressed. I drank a bottle of wine because I was missing my kids and feeling all alone and humiliated about what my life had become. One of the hardest steps I had to take was forcing myself to look at myself in the mirror and have an honest talk about where this behavior was going to lead me. Most likely into even further pain, health and financial circumstances. If I didn't change, I might even end up in a downward spiral, and I didn't want to give my kids that memory of me. I didn't want to allow the pain of my circumstances to win.

I remember staring at myself in the mirror in that new home, completely alone, then taking a bunch of photos of myself staring back. For some reason, I wanted to remember what this moment felt like. As I looked at those photos, I kept thinking, "Who the heck even are you?" and "What do you even want?"

I was so afraid to take the first step. One of the first thoughts I had was, "I don't have time to focus on myself, I have kids to take care of, a business to run, and a life that's falling apart." Makes sense, right? It felt like there was no room for self-care or healing amidst the chaos. But I realized that I couldn't be the mother, businesswoman, or person I wanted to be if I didn't make time for me first. I had to prioritize myself, even when it felt impossible.

I made the decision to invest in myself. I didn't know how to be alone without feeling lonely, so I started "dating" myself - taking myself out to dinner, to the movies, doing things that I hadn't allowed myself to enjoy because I was always too busy trying to be the "perfect wife" and mother. I had to learn how to enjoy my own company. It wasn't easy. There were days when I felt uncomfortable and awkward, but I pushed through because I knew I had to. I also knew I needed to rebuild my health on all levels - mentally, physically, and spiritually. But I was physically, emotionally and mentally exhausted from so much. I thought, "I can barely get out of bed some days. How am I supposed to take on the monumental task of rebuilding my life?"

I was so out of shape. Enough that even walking around the block got me winded, but I had to start somewhere. So, I forced myself to take small steps - literally. I started walking daily, sometimes just a few blocks, but I made the commitment to show up for myself. And that tiny step, day by day, started to build momentum. Once I got into the routine of walking, I started to set a goal. My first goal was 5,000 steps a morning. I even created a social media vlog and titled it the 5,000 Step Morning to hold me accountable to myself and whoever else wanted to join in. I started to read books in my spare time and listen to podcasts while walking that helped me think positively, even when I didn't want to. "Atomic Habits" helped me to implement some small habits first and then learn to adopt more on top of them via "habit stacking" over time. When you stack them, you multiply your results and anchor the new habit to the existing one.

I also began coaching real estate agents and investors in 2022. I loved working as a coach and seeing my students learn new strategies and help them become better at their craft. It felt good to be useful in this way since I have always loved the real estate industry. I built on the base of contacts I already had in the investing world, and it was starting to take off. However, with my income being solely my own, I struggled to find investment opportunities in a new place, and I didn't have the same contacts I had built up over decades in my old hometown. I had all these skills and was running into walls to be able to use them myself, so coaching others what I know was keeping me sharp and connected.

I was so focused on improving my health that I lost sight of what to prioritize. All I wanted was to work on myself without stressing over money, finding coaching clients, or chasing investment properties. But when my coaching income didn't skyrocket right away, doubt crept in. I felt the pressure from people around me suggesting I return to a more "stable" job for a little while, until my kids were older and more independent. Eventually, I let it get to me when I was offered an opportunity to return to my previous employer. I went back to my role in strategic business development, recruiting and offering workforce solutions in higher education and healthcare for a year. Most days, I was miserable. Not because I didn't enjoy the work itself, but because the constantly shifting schedule and heavy travel demands were more than I or my little family could manage. I was also terrified I'd slip back into old habits. It felt like I was moving backward instead of forward.

When we lose our way, it can often cause us to fall a few steps back or lose ground we've gained. When we wander, we travel the same path we've visited before and sometimes expect different results. Sometimes wilderness requires us to be still and wait.

Wandering in the Wilderness: Monica's Story of Transformation

Monica was a classically trained musician and teacher and had been married for almost 10 years when her wilderness season began as a storm she didn't see coming, marked by a cascade of losses that unraveled her life. Her journey through the wilderness was one of profound hardships, from divorce and financial ruin to the heartbreaking loss of her mother, ultimately leading her into homelessness. Yet beneath the struggles is a story of resilience, resourcefulness, and strength.

Monica's challenges seemed to come all at once. A painful divorce in 2015 from a narcissistic partner left her emotionally drained, and her financial stability crumbled when her ex-husband stopped paying the mortgage on their home, forcing her into foreclosure. At the same time, she lost her mother, which was a devastating blow that compounded her grief. "I felt like everything that could go wrong was happening all at once," Monica recalled. "It was overwhelming to lose my marriage, my home, and my mother all within such a short period."

Her divorce brought sharp clarity to patterns she had endured for years. "I grew up wired to think narcissistic behavior was normal," Monica admitted. "Healthy relationships felt foreign to me." The weight of her past collided with her present, leaving her stuck in a cycle of self-doubt and emotional exhaustion.

The foreclosure of her home left Monica with no choice but to live in her van for three years. Those years, she said, were the most humbling of her life. "Homelessness isn't just about not having a house," she shared. "It's about feeling unseen, unwelcome, and disconnected." Monica parked in store lots, relied on the kindness of strangers, and fought daily to maintain her dignity. She described being homeless as something like being the Ugly Duckling.

She recalls, "I felt like I was in the story of the Ugly Duckling, and going from place to place and not belonging and always being chased to the next place. And kept hearing, you can't stay here anymore. You can't be here anymore. All I kept hearing was. 'No, no, no, no, no!'"

Monica felt so low at times that she could understand why others in similar situations might give up and accept "no" as an answer. She acknowledged that many people experiencing homelessness, facing constant rejection and dead ends, might contemplate ending it all because they can't bear it any longer. "It's a lot," she said.

She continued to focus only on the one thing she could do in each moment. For her, it wasn't just about taking it day by day. It was often minute by minute to survive.

Despite the crushing circumstances, she found solace in small acts of kindness. A library director offered her a safe place to park. A compassionate police officer ensured she could rest without being disturbed. "It's those little moments of humanity that keep you going," she said. Even her dogs played a vital role, serving as her emotional anchors during the darkest days. "They were my lifeline," Monica said. "They gave me a reason to keep moving."

Like many wandering in the wilderness, Monica faced temptations that threatened to keep her stuck: doubts, distractions, and the urge to give up entirely. "There were days I felt like I couldn't take another step," she said. "The temptation to just quit was always there, but I couldn't let myself give in." One of her biggest challenges was being homeless during the whole COVID Pandemic.

Her turning point came not from a single moment of clarity but from the cumulative effect of refusing to give up. After a failed attempt to reconnect with family in Michigan, Monica found herself driving all night back to Rhinebeck, New York. "Something about New York felt alive to me," she said. "That drive back was when I realized I needed to rebuild my life on my terms."

Determined to regain stability, Monica threw herself into obtaining a real estate license and appraiser assistant license. She invested in training and equipment, overcoming countless obstacles along the way. "Every step felt like a fight," she admitted. "But focusing on what I could control in the moment helped me push forward."

Today, Monica has transitioned from merely surviving to rediscovering joy and creativity. She shares a home with a generous friend who has given her support while she builds her business. It has been a process of learning to even sleep peacefully again after having ongoing insomnia, but she now has a routine that helps her find solace. She takes pride in cooking, baking, returning to music and creating a life she loves. She even has a dream of one day helping other women who are similarly homeless with basic necessities like, food, shelter, a clean and safe place to maintain a sense of dignity and self-worth.

"The wilderness taught me to find beauty in the small things," she said. "It shaped me into someone stronger, someone who knows her worth."

Though her journey is ongoing, Monica's resilience shines through. She reflects on the progress she's made, knowing she is no longer the person she was during her marriage. "The wilderness shaped me, but it didn't define me," she said. "I'm stronger now, and I'm ready for whatever comes next."

Monica's story is a reminder that even in the darkest seasons, it's possible to find light and rebuild. "The wilderness grinds off your edges," she concluded, "but it also reveals the diamond underneath."

Lessons from Monica's Story

Monica's journey is a testament to the power of persistence, faith, and the refusal to quit. For those feeling stuck in their own wilderness, she offers this wisdom:

- **Take the Next Step:** "No matter how impossible it feels, every small action matters. Keep moving forward."

- **Refuse to Feel Small:** "Your situation does not define who you are. You have value. Remember, you are worthy of a better life."

- **Find Purposeful Movement:** Whether physical or mental, intentional action breaks the paralysis of despair.

PART 2: NAVIGATING THE WILDERNESS WITH YOUR **COMPASS**

THE COMPASS
EXPERT NAVIGATION

Navigating through the wilderness requires a reliable compass. For me, that compass has become a faith-led and intuitive process that I've observed through patterns and repeating themes in both my own experiences and the stories others have shared with me. These experiences all share a common theme: navigating a life-altering challenge, working through it, and ultimately overcoming it through a transformative process.

Trusting in God to guide me through uncertain times has proven invaluable in my life. Our inner compass helps us make decisions, find our way, and stay on course. Expert navigation involves trusting that we are being led, even when the path isn't clear.

As we explore the stories and chapters ahead, I will use the following foundation to outline the **COMPASS Framework** for navigating and thriving through Wilderness Seasons.

The COMPASS Framework: A Guiding Foundation

The **COMPASS Framework** is a guiding foundation for navigating Wilderness Seasons and finding strength through transformation. Each element represents a critical area for growth and resilience:

- **C - Community:**

Building and leaning into supportive relationships and networks. Community provides strength, accountability, and connection, reminding us that we are never alone in our journey.

- **O - Openness:**

A willingness to embrace change and release limiting beliefs. Openness is about letting go of fear and stepping into the unknown with faith, trust, and curiosity, allowing space for surrender to transformation and new opportunities to emerge.

- **M - Mindset:**

Building resilience and cultivating a growth-oriented mindset that reframes challenges as opportunities. This pillar focuses on rewiring your thoughts, empowering you to take intentional steps forward, and developing mental fitness to sustain momentum toward long-term transformation.

- **P - Purposeful Movement:**

Movement, both physical and mental- is the vehicle for transformation. Purposeful Movement emphasizes engaging in intentional practices, such as physical activity, structured routines, or mindful habits, to drive progress, create momentum, and align daily actions with your greater goals.

- **A - Accountability:**

Establishing systems for self-monitoring and progress tracking. Accountability keeps you grounded and focused, ensuring you follow through on commitments and stay aligned with your vision for growth.

- **S - Support:**

Drawing on mentors, tools, and resources to provide guidance and encouragement. Support is the foundation that sustains your journey through challenges and reinforces your resilience.

- **S - Self-Care:**

Prioritizing practices that nurture and renew your mind, body, and soul. Self-care is about more than indulgence; it's a critical pillar of growth and balance that allows you to show up fully in all areas of your life.

COMPASS FRAMEWORK

COMMUNITY

6
FINDING YOUR TRIBE

"As iron sharpens iron, so one person sharpens another". Proverbs 27:17

True belonging is the practice of believing in yourself so deeply that you can share your most authentic self with the world. It's about finding sacredness in both being part of something and standing strong on your own. As Brené Brown so wisely put it, "True belonging doesn't require you to change who you are; it requires you to be who you are."

That is where the concept of your tribe comes into play. Who you surround yourself with has a massive impact on your ability to heal, grow, and move forward. These people influence your mindset, your habits, and your overall outlook on life. If you are going through a major life transition, like divorce, illness or loss, maintaining the same circle you had before may not always serve you. Your life has shifted, and so must the people you allow access to your heart and energy.

Covid created patterns of isolation in our world. So many people have lost the art of being able to form good, quality relationships. We have become a society self-protected but silently and desperately lonely. People need people but the enemy loves to isolate us. We tend to feel like we're bothering people or are a burden when we *gasp* ask for help. Do you know what Jesus says in Matthew 11:28? *"Come to Me those of you who are heavy laden and burdened, for I will give you rest".*

How does God do this? Often through His people. But here's the catch, we must learn to reconnect with others before they can truly show up for us in the ways we need. It's a two-part solution: **an action followed by a response**.

"Come to Me" means we take that first vulnerable step. We turn toward God and toward others.

"I will give you rest" is His promise of what follows. He brings comfort, connection, and peace.

But connection does not happen without courage.

And rest rarely comes without reaching.

Your tribe will not always find you. Sometimes, you have to open the door first. Let others in. Let God use them. Healing often happens in the presence of community.

When my life fell into chaos during my divorce, I lost some relationships along the way. But I also experienced family and friends showing up for me in ways I can never repay. Late-night texts and phone calls; caring hearts who prayed with me and helped me discern truth from fiction; my therapist who patiently guided me through trauma and healing one day at a time; supportive Zoom calls with friends from my mastermind group; and a mentor or two who stood fiercely by my side, diving deep into spiritual battles and storming heaven's gates alongside me.

Church friends helped me pack up my home. Heartfelt prayers poured in from family and friends. And countless small acts of kindness reminded me I wasn't completely alone. My mother showed up at my doorstep, offering her quiet presence and unwavering love. Some went out of their way to make sure I felt seen and heard, even cracking jokes to lift my spirits when my face was puffy, covered in tears and boogers, and I hadn't showered in more hours than I care to admit.

But not everyone stayed.

Some of the losses were friendships, family members, and even people from church. Some couldn't handle the changes I was going through. Others didn't know the full story and made assumptions. A few simply no longer aligned with the woman I was becoming, especially after I moved to another state.

Rebuilding my community was something I had to do with intention, and honestly, it was terrifying. Vulnerability is hard, especially when you're already feeling broken. But I knew isolation wasn't the answer, so I pushed myself to step out of my comfort zone.

Once I committed to healing, I started showing up at networking events, in community spaces, and in groups where I could potentially belong. I even began creating spaces of my own. I surrounded myself with people who uplifted me, who were either on similar healing journeys or already walking the path I wanted to follow.

And when I came across someone who was struggling or not quite where I was yet, but clearly wanted to heal, I found myself coming back to a place where I could gently encourage them. I was able to connect in an authentic way and point them toward the direction I was heading. If they chose to come along, that was the greatest gift of all. Healing is contagious.

You see, it is not only about finding friends; it is about finding *good* friends. Your tribe should consist of people who challenge you, inspire you, and call you out on your

"B.S." when you need it. They are the ones who keep you accountable and help you grow. I've learned to reflect on the energy I feel when I'm around someone. Does this person leave me feeling drained or inspired? Do they encourage me to move forward or keep me stuck in the past? Do they speak life over me when I share something hard, or do they make me feel guilt, shame, or excluded for not being perfect or healing the way they think I should?

The people you spend time with shape your mindset and behavior. I once had a friend who was incredibly driven, always working toward her goals and radiating energy. I also had another friend who was more sedentary, content with where life had taken her. While I loved them both, it became clear that spending more time with the driven friend aligned better with the life I wanted to build. Her energy inspired me to push harder, while the other left me feeling static and stationary.

Sometimes it has nothing to do with the other person. Sometimes just being around them reminds you too much of who you used to be or the painful season you knew them through. When you're trying to grow past that version of yourself, you might need to take a break and return to the relationship when you feel more grounded. If you're not walking away but simply making space to grow, a true friend will understand. They'll hold that space and welcome you back with an open door when the time is right.

One of my dearest friends and I went through difficult personal seasons during separate times throughout our friendship. We gave each other space to heal but also made sure each other knew we understood that each other's seasons required us to focus our attention on what we were dealing with directly in front of us while still showing up for each other in ways that mattered but were respectful boundary wise. Our friendship has grown with grace, honesty, respect, trust, and just the right amount of sass when needed. You know it's the real deal when they show up to move heavy exercise equipment for you while all your life's belongings are packed up inside of a storage container while you're in the middle of moving because you are getting divorced. Another dear friend and I went through some challenging life seasons together (and real estate transactions) over many years and was the one who took my poor COVID chickens and rehomed them with her family for me. That's taking chicken math to a whole new level (chicken people will get this joke, for everyone else, just nod and smile).

This doesn't mean you have to cut people out of your life entirely, but it does mean being mindful of how much access you allow them to have. It's like the book "Up the Mood Elevator" in which Larry Senn describes how people can either lift you up or bring you down. Pay attention to how you feel after spending time with someone. If you feel drained, it may be time to reevaluate how much time and energy you invest in that relationship.

One of the most transformative steps I took after my divorce was intentionally seeking out supportive communities and serving others. I had already been coaching and consulting others in my business, but I added separation and divorce coaching to the services I offered as a life and business coach to help others with what I'd learned through my experience. I also started a walking group for women to help me find new friends in my new community. After joining a new church, I met with my pastors and got involved. I chose to facilitate a separation and divorce recovery small group for women, and helped launch a local single moms' outreach community to support other moms raising kids on their own. These connections not only helped me feel less isolated but also gave me opportunities to serve others. It's amazing how helping someone else can fill your own cup. When you shift your focus from your own pain to supporting others, it creates a sense of purpose and healing.

For one woman I worked with, community became her lifeline after her separation. She shared with me the devastation of learning her ex-husband was engaged to the woman he had been unfaithful with. It was a painful blow, but staying anchored in her new tribe kept her moving forward. The women she surrounded herself with had been through similar experiences and helped her see that there was light on the other side. She started to believe that she, too, could rebuild her life and find joy again.

Your body and emotions will often give you signals about the people in your life. Pay attention to how someone makes you feel, not just in the moment but afterward. Do you feel energized, peaceful, or inspired? Or do you feel drained, tense, or stuck? These cues are invaluable when deciding who belongs in your life.

Boundaries are another critical piece of the puzzle. It's not easy, especially when you love someone or have a long history with them. However, boundaries aren't about shutting people out; they're about protecting your peace and ensuring your relationships serve your growth. Sometimes it means saying no to plans or limiting your interactions with someone who brings negativity into your life. Other times, it's about communicating clearly what you need and expect from those closest to you.

As I have worked through my own journey, I've learned the importance of alignment. When life feels out of balance, it is often because we are giving too much time and energy to things or people that don't reflect our goals and values.

Recently, I found myself overwhelmed by commitments to an event I was planning. It was a great idea, but it wasn't the right time. I stepped back, adjusted the timeline, and felt an immediate sense of relief. That one decision freed me up to focus on other priorities without feeling stretched too thin.

Sometimes alignment means collaborating with someone on a project instead of trying to do it all myself. And sometimes it means hiring someone else to take it off my plate entirely. For someone like me, a Type A personality with a side of neuro-spicy ADD tendencies, delegation used to feel like handing over a toddler to a stranger with no instructions and hoping for the best. I always worried no one would do it the way I wanted, or worse, that I would lose my precious toddler baby project.

Since reading *Who Not How* by Dan Sullivan and Dr. Benjamin Hardy, and *Buy Back Your Time* by Dan Martell, I am finally starting to see what it looks like to actually apply those principles. It is definitely easier to highlight and underline ideas in a book than to implement them in real life. But letting go, even little by little, has brought me more freedom than I expected. Fellow business owners will know exactly what I mean.

This same principle applies to your relationships. It's not about cutting people out entirely but knowing how much time and energy to allocate to each person based on how they align with your current needs and goals.

Finding your tribe isn't merely about surrounding yourself with people who make you feel good; it's about finding those who help you grow. The women in my walking groups, church groups, and coaching sessions have reminded me repeatedly of the power of shared experiences. Seeing someone else who navigates a tough season and comes out stronger gives hope and perspective. It's a beautiful exchange. Those further along in their journey can offer guidance, while those just starting out remind us of how far we've come.

If you're in a season of transition, take inventory of your community and close tribe. Who lifts you up? Who challenges you to be better? Who shares your vision for the future? And, just as importantly, who do you need to step back from to protect your peace and stay focused on your path? True belonging starts with believing in yourself and surrounding yourself with people who reflect and reinforce that belief. Together, you'll navigate the wilderness and move closer to the life you're meant to live.

7
CONNECTIONS

Layla's Journey to Healing and Connection

Layla's story begins in deep pain, shaped by a childhood filled with dysfunction and survival. She was born into a chaotic home. Her father hid his sexuality, and her mother practiced witchcraft. Stability, guidance, and love were nowhere to be found.

As the third of nine children, Layla carried responsibilities far beyond her years, often caring for her younger siblings while still a child herself. With no real support system, she was forced to scavenge through dumpsters for food and clothing, doing whatever it took to get by.

The absence of safety and nurturing left a lasting imprint, instilling a deep sense of scarcity, mistrust, and disconnection that would follow her long after those early years.

"I grew up believing that chaos and survival were normal," Layla recalls. "Healthy relationships and stability were foreign concepts."

She spent much of her life in fight-or-flight mode, responding to the world in the only way she knew how: by keeping herself guarded, isolated, and in control. Her childhood wounds laid the groundwork for patterns of self-destructive relationships and behaviors that carried into adulthood. It wasn't until her thirties, when her body began to shut down, that she realized just how deep the damage had gone.

At first, she didn't understand what was happening to her. She did everything she had been told to do. She worked out, ate well, and appeared put-together, but none of it mattered. Her health was deteriorating, and no doctor could pinpoint why. The reality was that years of trauma, neglect, and dysfunctional relationships had taken their toll. The deeper she dug into her condition, the more she realized that her external struggles were merely symptoms of a much greater internal battle.

"I finally understood that my body was responding to everything I had buried inside of me. The emotional wounds, the stress, the dysfunction. It was all manifesting physically," she shared.

Her breaking point came when she collapsed in exhaustion, barely able to function. It was then that she had to make a choice. She could continue down the same road of self-denial and survival or step into a completely new path, one that required surrender.

Layla realized she couldn't heal while holding onto the very things that had broken her. She described the overwhelming need to shed the patterns that kept her stuck. She had spent years in survival mode, but surviving was no longer enough. She needed to heal.

This meant confronting her own patterns, habits, and the toxic cycles she had unknowingly repeated. It meant releasing the identity of survival and embracing a new way of living. It meant learning to trust for the first time in her life.

One of the most profound steps in her journey was legally changing her name to Layla Grace. It was a symbolic declaration that she was stepping into a new season, a new identity, and a new way of being. It wasn't about escaping her past. It was about fully stepping into who she was always meant to be in God's love.

Perhaps the most transformative part of Layla's healing was learning the value of community and relationships. Having grown up in isolation, she had always believed that trusting people was dangerous. But as she began working through ACA (Adult Children of Alcoholics) and her 12-step program, she discovered something life-changing. We don't heal in isolation.

"For years, I kept people at arm's length, believing that I could only rely on myself," Layla said. "But I learned that healing requires connection."

Building a new, strong, personal community was one of the hardest but most necessary steps in her journey. She had to evaluate the relationships in her life and intentionally choose the ones that would support her growth. It was no longer about who had been there the longest, but rather who could walk with her in the direction she was going.

"Trust was something I had to practice, step by step," she said. "Even something as simple as being truthful in a text message was a huge leap for me at first."

She slowly learned to differentiate between relationships that drained her and those that fueled her. Some connections naturally faded, while others deepened as she allowed herself to be vulnerable in safe spaces.

She found incredible support in her faith community, where people held space for her without judgment. For the first time in her life, she wasn't trying to earn love. She was simply receiving it.

"Having people who genuinely saw me, who cared and didn't judge, helped me rediscover my worth," she shared.

Layla's healing wasn't just physical or emotional. It was deeply spiritual. She realized that she had spent years trying to control her life out of fear rather than trusting in God's provision and plan.

"I had spent years leading others to Jesus, but I lacked true intimacy with Him myself," she admitted. "I had to repent for living out of self-will and learn how to trust God's guidance."

This shift in perspective changed everything. Instead of trying to force outcomes, she began to surrender daily. She would wake up each morning and ask God what He wanted from her that day. Even in the smallest tasks, she sought His guidance.

This new way of living brought clarity, direction, and a sense of peace she had never known before. Instead of feeling lost and unworthy, she began to walk in confidence, knowing she was exactly where she needed to be.

Layla's transformation didn't happen overnight. She had to unlearn decades of survival-based habits and embrace the slow, steady process of healing. She describes it as moving through three phases: hurting, healing, and helping.

"You can't rush through it," she says. "Each season has a purpose."

She made radical self-care a priority. This didn't just mean bubble baths and rest. It meant consciously choosing what she consumed, what she surrounded herself with, and what thoughts she allowed in her mind.

She visualized a better future by creating a vision board and practicing affirmations. She would ask herself daily, "What if it all worked out?" That simple question reframed her thinking from fear to possibility.

Today, Layla's life is a testament to the power of change, faith, and intentional relationships. She no longer sees herself as a victim of her past but as a woman who has been restored, empowered, and aligned with her purpose.

She built a thriving marriage and business with her husband, both centered around faith, healing, and service. Together, they help others find health, wealth, and transformation through relationships.

"I worked hard to change my environment, my personal community, and my mindset," Layla said. "Now, I get to help others do the same."

Her story is a powerful reminder that who we surround ourselves with matters. The impact of those you choose to keep in your life can either keep you stuck or propel you forward.

For anyone feeling lost in their own wilderness, Layla offers this advice:

- **Start Small**: Begin with the basics, like nourishing your body and mind with small, intentional acts of self-care.

- **Find Your Tribe**: Surround yourself with people who uplift and support you. Community is essential to healing.

- **Surrender to God's Plan**: Let go of self-will and trust that God has a purpose for your life, even in the wilderness.

- **Embrace the Process**: Healing takes time. Give yourself grace and patience as you move through the seasons of hurting, healing, and helping.

Layla's journey is a living testament to what happens when we choose faith over fear, trust over control, and connection over isolation.

Her life was once defined by survival, but today, she is thriving, whole, healed, and aligned with God's purpose.

And that same transformation is available to you.

COMPASS FRAMEWORK

OPENNESS

8

FAITH: A COMPASS THROUGH THE STORM

"Now faith is the substance of things hoped for, the evidence of things not seen." Hebrews 11:1 KJV

Faith is essential. Faith that comes from within yourself, above all. And faith that you can, and deserve to, when necessary, move forward to heal, grow, and reclaim your life, no matter where you are on your journey of belief.

Let me start by being honest. I have struggled with my faith. Big time. I've walked away from churches because I confused imperfect people with a perfect God. I let their failures shape my view of Him, and for a while, it pulled me away. I've misinterpreted people's intentions and communications, and I've probably done the same to others without realizing it. Through these experiences, I've learned an important lesson: my accountability must be to God first and people second.

You may be struggling with your faith, too. While no human can solve the great mystery of God, my hope is that you experience knowing that whatever season you're in, you see and feel the love of God and His Wisdom throughout these seasons. God truly loves you. His love is available to you, should you choose to receive it.

You may be struggling with people, too. People you

love and who love you, but who are hurting, confused, angry, bitter, or just stuck in their own mess. People who think life has to be done *this* way or *that* way, or else it's not right. Maybe you've got parents who still don't treat you like an adult, even though you've been out on your own for years. You might be raising kids of your own. Maybe you don't have children, but you're out here paying bills, making big life decisions, or serving your country.

When my son enlisted in the military at 19 and was suddenly stationed overseas for two years, it hit me. He was old enough to fight and possibly die for our country, yet I still saw him as my baby. That transition was hard. It made me realize how much we all wrestle with letting people grow up and how often people wrestle with letting *us* grow up, too.

Sometimes the tension runs deeper into your faith or belief systems. Maybe your family believes differently about God. Maybe some don't believe at all. And when those topics come up? Let's just say... holiday dinners can get real uncomfortable, real fast. You're not alone in that.

You might also be carrying some hurt from church or religious communities. I've come to realize that while pastors and leaders are human, we sometimes treat them like they're not. We put them on pedestals. We hand them authority to tell us what our relationship with God *should* look like, how to live, how to worship, how to measure if we're doing it "right." And all of it? Based on *their* interpretation of scripture.

But here's the truth: pastors, elders, church leaders, friends in the pew, people who've left church, and people who've never stepped foot in one... we're all just people.

We all fall short. We all get it wrong from time to time. And we all need grace, which is why Jesus came. Every single one of us is figuring it out as we go. None of us are too far gone. And all of us are in need of a little more compassion—for others and for ourselves. If only we could stop trying to pretend everything's fine all the time to keep up appearances. Eventually, it all comes falling down around us. Big lesson learned there for me. I've got a tee-shirt as president of that club, if you catch my drift.

And listen, yes, pastors and ministers are human just like the rest of us. But that role they've been called to? It's a big one. It's not just a title; it's a responsibility. The Bible is clear that God takes spiritual leadership seriously. James 3:1 says not many should become teachers because those who do are held to a stricter standard. That's not nothing.

We should absolutely be praying for our pastors. Leading people, especially in faith, is no small task. And when they show up with integrity, humility, and truth, we need to honor that. Celebrate it. Support it.

I have a brother who is a minister. Don't get me wrong, he's a man of God, but to me he's still my brother and is also still husband to his wife and dad to his kids. We joke, we reminisce, we still argue about who's Mom's favorite (obviously me, *duh*). The Ministry doesn't erase your sibling card. Watching someone I love walking out his calling with serious regard for both the responsibility and the weight of it has given me even more perspective. I've seen both the beautiful and the difficult sides of ministry, and I know how much heart and humility it takes to do it well.

But that doesn't mean we turn a blind eye when leadership goes sideways. Being called doesn't mean being above correction. And it definitely doesn't mean replacing your relationship with God with someone else's opinion about Him. That's why it matters so much to know the Word for yourself. Let God's voice be the loudest one in your life, even if someone in a pulpit let you down.

A great resource that helped me process this well is a book my own pastor recently recommended to our church: *Hope After Church Hurt* by Joe Dobbins. It's a short and powerful read that helps you heal, forgive, and reconnect with God after experiencing pain within a church setting. If you've been there, this book might meet you right where you are.

And sometimes, part of that compassion is realizing that the people we once looked up to - parents, mentors, elders - don't always have it all together. As kids, we assume the adults around us have all the answers. But as we grow up, we start to see their cracks, too. I've written earlier in this book about a moment I had with my dad, how I used to carry pain around the fact that he never defended me when I was younger. But now, I understand why. He wasn't equipped. He wasn't healthy. He was young, unstable, and battling his own demons. He was using drugs and alcohol and functioning from a place of survival, not wisdom or strength. That doesn't erase the hurt, but it does shift the lens. It helps us extend grace when we realize they were just people trying to get through their own mess, too.

We're all on a journey. And we all shift our perspective at different times in life, depending on the lens we're looking through. Some of us are on fire for God, at the beginning of our faith journey, and can't understand why everyone doesn't see the miracle of salvation as clearly as we do. Some are in the messy middle-facing real trials, temptations, and even wars. And some have made it through to the other side. They carry a calm, steady faith that only comes from being tested, refined, and seasoned by the storms of life. They've run the race. They've fought through doubt. And they have stayed the course.

As scripture reminds us, *"When I was a child, I spoke like a child, I thought like a child, I reasoned like a child. When I became a man, I gave up childish ways."* (1 Corinthians 13:11). We don't all mature at the same pace, and that's okay. God's not in a rush with us. But He *is* always inviting us closer.

So, wherever you are, whether you're questioning everything, holding on by a thread, or walking with a peace that passes understanding...God's grace still meets you there.

I've come to realize that while leaders in formal places of worship are human, we, as a society often grant them "god-like" authority. We give them platforms and permissions to dictate how we should have a relationship with the divine Creator or how to live our lives, based on their interpretation of the Bible. Ministers, church leaders, elders, and congregants are all imperfect people. So are those who don't believe in God at all. ALL of us fall short, sin, and make mistakes. We ALL need redemption because of it.

There was only one perfect Human, and He's the only one I ultimately answer to at the end of my days. His Word tells me to love others as He has loved us, and that's what I strive to do. Some days, I succeed. Other days, I fail miserably, even with the best of intentions. I can understand how hard it is to walk upright and blameless when I am covered in imperfection.

Sometimes "church people" showed up for my highest highs but left me alone in my lowest lows. Other times, I became so connected to the idea of a church "family" that I forgot my own family took precedence. I'd been preached at so hard to "drop everything" for a call to help or volunteer that I felt resentful and unfairly treated. After my divorce, I took time off from "church life" to heal from the hurt I'd experienced with not just one but two churches I had been part of.

This is why so many believers leave the church or their faith altogether. They confuse the actions of people with God. I know there are many good people in churches. For the most part, we're all humans trying to do good for good reasons. But we all have bad days, get sick, and go through wilderness seasons of our own, which can unintentionally inflict deep damage on others.

I don't know if you've noticed lately, but a lot of people are skeptical, agnostic, or outright angry about God. Many struggle to understand why bad things happen to good people and why good things seem to happen to bad people.

I've experienced being let down during difficult times by ministry leaders, despite their good intentions. My biggest mistake was putting them on a pedestal and allowing them to interpret what I needed from God, rather than trusting my own instincts and listening inwardly for His guidance. This included being encouraged to stay in a marriage that was horribly broken and unhealthy.

If you're in an unhealthy marriage and questioning whether God would "allow" you to leave, especially under counsel from religious leadership, I highly recommend reading Natalie Hoffman's *"Is It Me? Making Sense of Your Confusing Marriage."* It offers empathetic insights that may help you find direction in such a challenging situation.

I've also taken accountability for my role in failed relationships, whether in marriage, church, family, or friendships. Doing a self-inventory required me to ask hard questions about my actions, responsibilities, and perceptions. I wasn't prepared to acknowledge my own shortcomings at first, but I've learned to give myself grace, reflect, and grow from my failures. This process has taught me about transformation, mindset, forgiveness, self-discovery, and recovery; lessons I am excited to share with you. I encourage you to explore this journey for yourself. Another resource in alignment with Hoffman's is Patrick Weaver Ministries. His Facebook page has given me insight through some difficult conversations with myself and others around infidelity, the church and boundaries.

I've since returned to a new church and am actively involved in serving others. It brings me joy. But I now check my internal temperature regularly to ensure I'm not becoming overly dependent on the church, its leadership, or its congregants. I focus on serving with a heart of humility and giving credit to God alone for what I do. I accept counsel when needed but align my decisions with God's Word and His Holy Spirit.

I've learned to trust God and myself while maintaining healthy boundaries with others. I also try not to take myself or others too seriously. Ego and selfish desires can muddy decision-making, and I remind myself to keep God at the center. Thankfully, His grace is patient when I miss His direction.

As someone who has walked through the wilderness, I've come to believe that seasons of struggle have purpose. I'm not a perfect Christian. Only one of those exists, and I am not Him. I'm an Italian girl (half Sicilian to boot- pun intended) from New Jersey, who still slips up and cusses when I forget myself. Because of this, I owe my accountability partner a $10 bill every time I fall out of line. She enjoys the fruit of my mouth's misfortune. But seriously, none of us are without sin. (Romans 3:10).

My pastor recently preached a sermon on keeping our language aligned with living a holy life. As a life coach who teaches my clients about the power of words, it hit home for me. I nearly slid out of my seat, sure he was looking right at me and shaking his head. He has a fabulous sense of humor, for which I am grateful.

I have as many valleys as I do mountaintops on this journey. And while my ex-husband calls my faith-filled family and friends "Water Walkers," suggesting we think we're perfect, I've come to take it as a compliment. I know I'm perfectly imperfect, redeemed by God's forgiveness, and walking in His promises for my life, which are undeserved but freely given by a merciful Father who loves me.

Faith is the compass that keeps me moving forward. I want the kind of faith Peter had when he stepped out of the boat to walk on water. Believe me, I've tried. Recently on a trip to Hawaii, I saw the size of the waves and immediately shook with doubt and fear, lacking even more faith that I could walk on them. When I get to Heaven, one of my first adventures will be surfing Hawaii-sized waves with no board. In the meantime, I'm thinking of designing some "Water Walker" shirts and hats. Until then, I'm learning to step out in faith in smaller ways, one decision at a time, even when it still feels a little wobbly.

How You Can Cultivate Openness:

Pray Honestly: Tell God your fears and doubts. Invite Him into the hardest parts of your story. Talk to Him like you're talking to your best friend. He wants that kind of relationship with you. Jesus even said, *"I no longer call you servants... I have called you friends"* (John 15:15).

Anchor in Scripture: Find verses that remind you of God's promises and repeat them when fear creeps in. One of my favorite verses to speak over myself when fear creeps in is 2 Timothy 1:7 *"For God has not given us a spirit of fear, but of power and of love and of a sound mind."* I don't always feel powerful or clear-headed in the moment, but this verse reminds me of what *is* mine in Him, and I keep speaking it until it sinks in.

Take Small Steps of Faith: Trust doesn't always look like big leaps. It's often found in the small, consistent steps forward.

9

FASTING

"Trust in the Lord with all your heart and lean not on your own understanding; in all your ways submit to him, and he will make your paths straight" Proverbs 3:5-6 NIV

When most people hear the word *fasting*, they either think of crash diets, detox trends, or someone skipping meals and calling it holy. Let's be real. Fasting has gotten a reputation for being either a super-spiritual mystery or just a fancy word for being hungry and grumpy.

But here's the thing: you've probably practiced some form of fasting without even realizing it. Ever taken a break from social media because it was draining your energy? Chosen to pause on Netflix binges to clear your head? Maybe you've skipped that nightly glass of wine to reset. That's fasting in its simplest form. Stepping away from something to make space for something better.

Fasting isn't about punishment or proving how strong you are. It's about *purpose*. It's about hitting pause on the things that distract, comfort, or even control us, so we can refocus—on God, on clarity, on what actually matters. Whether you've never fasted a day in your life or you've done a 21-day Daniel Fast with your church, this isn't about rules. It's about reconnecting with your spirit, your purpose, and yes, with God.

So, before you start thinking this is some "super-saint" practice reserved for pastors and people who only drink green juice, take a breath. You might find fasting is more familiar, and more freeing, than you ever expected.

In wilderness seasons, fasting can be a powerful practice. It's not just about abstaining from food; it is about creating space for spiritual nourishment and trusting God to sustain us. As we step away from the things that usually keep us going, we open ourselves to be "fed" by His Word and guided more clearly. Fasting helps clear away distractions, sharpen our focus on what truly matters, and deepen our connection with God. It also teaches us to rely on something greater than our usual comforts and routines.

Even though fasting is more of a spiritual practice, there are people and faiths that fast in a variety of ways. When we intentionally withhold something that may be distracting us from whatever we want our focus to be, taking that thing away in order so that we can get closer to our own heart, our own truth, or God, is important. If you have a health issue, and are considering fasting from food, consult your doctor before doing so.

Fasting is a personal decision and commitment. If you choose to fast and it is medically safe for you, the following are potential benefits. There are physical benefits such as weight loss, releasing toxins, resetting our digestive system, and regulating our metabolism. Mentally, it can help with exercising a level of self-control and discipline. I personally use intermittent fasting as a regular practice with my diet and combined with healthy whole foods, exercise and water, it has aided me with losing over 60lbs since January of 2023.

St. Augustine said, "Fasting cleanses the soul, raises the mind, subjects one's flesh to the spirit, renders the heart contrite and humble, [and] scatters the clouds of concupiscence". The spiritual benefits of fasting can be that it helps you resist temptation and come face to face with the things that once controlled you. It also helps with building trust with God by relying on Him to strengthen you during your fast. It also helps you when you pray, to be less distracted and makes prayer life more powerful. (see Luke 2:37, Ezra 8:21, Nehemiah 1:4, and Acts 14:23).

While many people fast from food, that is not the only thing from which you can fast. Alcohol, social media, anything that triggers us from reaching a goal or finding clarity. You can even use something as simple as music. There may be songs that, when you focus on the lyrics, bring back memories, or can cause you to think of a person or place which triggers us to fall into an unhealthy pattern.

If you have never fasted before, I'd recommend you start slow, journaling while doing it to keep track of how you feel, what you experience and any revelations or breakthroughs that occur. Did you notice a difference? Do you feel stronger? When I fast, I find it to be empowering and like I've won a marathon after doing it. I've fasted during seasons in collaboration with my church body as according to Joel 2:12-15. I love that God instructs us to fast as a way of turning our hearts to Him in an act of repentance, yielding a way of drawing us closer.

And so, when you take something away, it allows room for something else to grow and to come into your focus. Whatever it is you are trying to get clarity on, fasting can certainly help with it.

As I mentioned, at the beginning of 2023, after having succumbed to my fears and anxieties about being on my own, I decided to return to my W2 job. I was incredibly grateful to have had the opportunity to have done it at the time. It provided me with a more stable income, and benefits for my daughters. It also helped me qualify for a mortgage to buy the house I am grateful to now call my home. My son was 26 at the time and fully self-sufficient. He was living out of state serving the remainder of his time in the military before coming home to live with us to finish his college degree, so the new home would provide enough space for all three of my children to be with me.

My sister-in-law, knowing I didn't want to return to that field, suggested this opportunity could be a temporary provision for now, or what the bible refers to as a "ram in the thicket". The phrase comes from a story in Genesis, where Abraham is about to sacrifice his son Isaac, but at the last moment, God provided a ram caught in a thicket as a substitute offering. It symbolizes divine intervention and unexpected provision in a time of need. She wasn't telling me to take the job or claiming it was some divine calling in business casual. She simply offered a thoughtful perspective that sometimes God provides something to sustain us for now, even if it is not the forever plan. And hey, sometimes a ram is just there to keep you from losing your mind - or your health insurance.

As grateful as I was for the solutions the job provided, I was not happy about returning to corporate life. I did not feel like I was making the kind of impact I had when coaching and serving others on my own. By January of 2024, I was miserable, exhausted, and deeply discouraged about where I was in my career.

In the beginning, it seemed like travel would decrease and there'd be room for growth, especially with my background in leadership. But after applying for two leadership roles and watching them go to others who seemed already positioned for the roles, discouragement crept in fast. I felt myself slipping into a downward spiral. I didn't want to stay stuck in a dead-end position I had already mastered years ago, one that no longer challenged me.

At home, my daughters were feeling the strain, too. They were struggling emotionally from both my absence and their father's distance. I couldn't keep up with it all, and I knew something had to change if I wanted to protect my mental and physical health.

Every new year, my church hosts a 21-day time of corporate prayer, consecration and fasting called "Sacred Season". I had never fasted in this way. The most I had ever done were personal fasts, but none had lasted more than a day or two at most.

So, I did it. I fasted my favorite meal for 21 days and for the last 3 of those days, I fasted completely only with water and coffee. I donated to church in faith that God would provide me with an answer on what to do next.

What started with a leap of faith and a fast has grown into a business that finally feels like *me*. I've always known I wasn't built for just one lane. My need for creativity, diversity, meaningful connection, and let's be honest, a mix of strategy and soul, was never a flaw. It's exactly how God wired me to serve.

Through fasting, God didn't just give me clarity. He reminded me that everything truly is *figureoutable*. I had first read Marie Forleo's book, **Everything is Figureoutable**, back in 2021 when I was starting my real estate investing journey. At the time, it motivated me, but during that quiet, focused time with God in 2024, the message clicked in a much deeper way. He showed me how to apply what I'd learned not just in business, but in life.

God gave me permission to fully embrace being **multi-passionate**. I didn't have to choose one path or limit how I served. I could align every passion, every skill, and every lesson with His purpose and create something that reflected *all* of who He designed me to be. But more importantly, He reminded me of **who** I was called to serve first, my family.

One of the biggest reasons I left my job wasn't just to build a business I loved, but to be **present**. My children may be older, ranging from teens to their twenties, but they still need their mom. Stepping into this calling meant I could be more accessible, more available for the conversations, the guidance, or simply being home when they needed me most. No career accomplishment could ever replace that. Through **The Wilderness Compass**, God made a way for me to serve others while still showing up fully for the people who matter most.

Some days, that looks like coaching women through personal breakthroughs, helping them rebuild confidence and direction after divorce, grief, or career shifts. Other days, it's guiding a business leader through team challenges, or working with an entrepreneur to design a strategy for growth that doesn't sacrifice their sanity.

I've had the opportunity to speak at conferences, share stories with single moms' groups, lead group coaching sessions for women on Zoom, and appear on podcasts to encourage others navigating life's toughest seasons. I get to pour into people, businesses, and communities in the most unique, creative, and purposeful ways, without borders.

It's never been about titles or programs. At the core, it's always been the same: helping people and teams find clarity, resilience, and purpose, and pairing that with real-world strategies to move forward when life or business feels overwhelming.

I share this because I am living proof that when you surrender your plans, trust God through the wilderness, and create space to listen, He'll lead you to a place where your gifts, passions, and purpose align better than you ever imagined.

Reflective Prompt:

Have you ever fasted before?

What is something you could fast from?

What do you need clarity on and how can it help you to have more focus on this thing?

10

MANNA

"But my God shall supply all your need according to his riches in glory by Christ Jesus." Philippians 4:19

"For I know the plans I have for you," declares the LORD, *"plans to prosper you and not to harm you, plans to give you hope and a future"* Jeremiah 29:11.

When the Israelites were in the desert, they received manna and quail from heaven to sustain them. You too can receive divine support and guidance from God and people He uses, and sometimes in unexpected places.

Many times, in our wilderness season, we go through stages of change in finances, change in living situations or changes in how we depend on being fed, clothed or housed. When something changes drastically, just trying to trust that no matter what, we will still have the ability to provide for ourselves and that somehow, we'll still make it through, can be challenging.

When we take a step of faith following a new direction, often we begin to be challenged in ways and can often question ourselves, doubt we heard God or think that we've made a mistake. Ever feel that way? I have. The challenges I've experienced in the last year that surround my career path have been some of the most I've ever gone through to date. Even though my new life began with many seasons of success, I have challenges just like everyone else and have my doubts at times.

To know we'll still be able to find those resources that we need is key. It just may look different than what we originally thought. But either way, somehow, some way, we hope and pray we will always find a way, right? That we will find some way to give us what we need at that moment. Being a good steward of our resources, and really making sure that we use them to the best of our ability can be challenging. It can be offsetting if you get a nice influx of money and then don't plan for rainy days because you become overindulgent or lack a solid budget. I've had this happen myself, where I've had a very, very bountiful season, and then have serious seasons of drought, like whoa, what's going on here? Goodness gracious, where'd that money go? That's up and down, up and down. This was often my pattern while in real estate. I'd have great months and months that were super slow. It was often a nail-biter of a career and at times it felt like feast or famine!

So, how do we find a way to be more consistent in trusting that we always will have what we need, as opposed to feeling lack, overabundance, or not feeling worthy of having too much or enough? How do we get our mind wrapped around those things and understand how to make sure that when those opportunities to make money come, we step into them? We pay attention to those things because sometimes we ask God to bring us income, and he sends it in the form of a person who's going to help us. He may ask us to write a book, or serve in ministry, or plant an idea for a business in our mind or connect us to a resource that can help us with inventing something. God mostly does not just open up the windows of heaven and throw down a fistful of dollars and make it rain on your life randomly. He wants you to partner with Him to encounter His Hand in your increase and prosperity.

Did you know God loves numbers? He's a stickler for attention to detail. Recently, I experienced a perfect example of God's provision and His attention to detail and numbers specifically. One Sunday morning, I was in church and during the time where the offering was being collected, I was challenged in a way I wasn't prepared for. I've been a giver and practiced tithing (offering 10% of my income to God) for decades. Since my divorce and fully being on my own, I have been stretched in my dependence on God in ways I've never imagined. I have found myself thinking "It's really just me now, 100% me, and I'm all in on this by myself to make sure I don't screw things up or mismanage my finances".

I have been faithfully pouring into this season, both in my work and through acts of obedience, trusting God as my ultimate provider. However, the progress of my business has been slower than anticipated, and unexpected expenses have added extra pressure. This has led me to reflect deeply on God's promises of provision and examine whether there are lessons I'm meant to learn at this moment, particularly about trust, stewardship, and my relationship with money.

That Sunday, during the offering time, I kept hearing the number 100 in my spirit. I thought, "Lord, that's not what my tithe should be, and I shouldn't be giving that much." I considered giving 50 instead, but the number 100 persisted. Reluctantly, I decided I would make the donation through my church's mobile app after the service, still feeling uncertain.

After the service, I went to the altar with my daughters as they prayed with the church prayer team. I prayed for them, ready to leave once they were done. But at the last moment, I felt the urgency to ask for prayer for myself.

When I approached the woman on the prayer team, she greeted me with a warm smile and asked what I needed prayer for. Though I had never met her before, her kindness put me at ease. I quietly explained that I needed clarity about whether I had truly heard God's direction in quitting my W2 job to fully commit to starting and running my business. I shared my desire for His blessing over this endeavor, knowing the impact it could have on many lives. I also mentioned the mental attacks I'd been facing, which at times felt overwhelming, making it a struggle to stay focused on the path ahead.

After she prayed, I thanked her and started to turn away. The next thing I knew, she tapped my shoulder, and I turned around and she told me to wait a second. She rushed over to her seat in the sanctuary and came back to me and handed me a fistful of money and said, "I don't know how much is there but is everything I had in my purse. God told me to sow this seed with you." I was uncomfortable accepting the money from her and told her she didn't have to do that, but she says she was being obedient. I realized I was still uncomfortable receiving money from people due to my struggle with confidence, feeling unworthy and not being valuable enough to charge my worth, and unable to receive and manage blessings with confidence and gratitude. I thanked her, took the money and walked out feeling convicted. I couldn't even count it until later. But I had such a strong feeling I already knew how much money was handed to me.

I got home and sure enough there was $100 sitting in my purse. Friend, if you don't think God is involved and interested in money, numbers or finances let me tell you, He is. He just demonstrated a specific numeric accuracy in my own personal spirit realm. He told me to get specific about how much money I want to earn and how much I should expect my business to make and to set some specific goals and action steps to align so He could start sending exactly what I need.

I needed this lesson. Even as a person who's been a believer for over 25 years and has been watching God provide for me and my family for all of it. I've also witnessed what happens when you step out of partnership with Him and what will occur when you try to do it all on your own or turn your back on Him completely, specifically when you have been called and have acknowledged that calling.

It doesn't end there. One week later my pastor was standing on stage as I entered the service (about 10 minutes after service started), and he was holding a woman's pocketbook on stage with him, and was demonstrating an example of a lesson on using God's gifts and things that God gives to us. The lesson went on to explain how to be a good steward of those things. Then he picked up the purse and used the example of how the $100 in the woman's purse he's holding doesn't belong to him, it belongs to her. He shared that it is the same concept when we ask God for provision, that the things He gives us to use belong to Him, how we are just stewards of those things.

Once the lesson ended, my pastor handed the purse back to the woman who it belonged to. To my astonishment, it was the same woman, who the week before had given me the $100. I just sat there in shock. I was asking myself, "How is this even a thing?" I know my pastor had no knowledge of anything that was going on, and I was walking in when he was doing the demonstration. It's not like either of them knew I was there or anything like that. After that, I was just very, very led to give $100 again that day, because that 100 kept showing up again. I'm being obedient to whatever it is that God's trying to teach me through this whole lesson. I have no idea how it's going to turn out, but I have had some whopper ideas come through my mind since that happened and I think it may be a result of me being more obedient in accepting provision and using my resources as He guides me to.

There are other times in my life when things have shown up inexplicably during times when I most needed them. When I was 26, during my first Thanksgiving as a single mother, I recall a woman from my church just showing up at my house with more groceries and housing supplies than I had ever imagined possible. Another woman and her husband blessed me two years later with free housing when I needed a place to live when I felt God leading me back to live closer to my family. She remains a dear friend and inspiration to this day. I've also witnessed some amazing blessings in my time where God has moved on the hearts of others to bless people in similar ways. Most recently, I saw two single mothers receive cars for FREE! If God can do these things for me, He can certainly do them for you!

Reflective Prompts:

- What area of your life are you seeking provision in?
- Have you had a hard time learning to trust God for provision?
- Have you felt like you doubted your ability to charge people what you are truly worth?

Rebuilding Through Openness: Linda's Story of Faith and Healing
▽90

Linda's journey began with a whirlwind romance that quickly turned into a tumultuous marriage. At just 20 years old, stationed in Germany, she married a man in the military, a functioning alcoholic whose charm masked deeper struggles. "He proposed to me under duress," Linda shared, reflecting on the early warning signs she didn't recognize at the time. Their marriage endured seven years of emotional highs and lows before a moment of devastating clarity arrived.

One day, Linda discovered her husband was involved with another woman. The betrayal hit her like a lightning bolt, shattering her sense of security. "He left, and I was left alone," she said, describing the intense loneliness and shock she felt. But the emotional pain didn't end there. What followed was a long, arduous battle for her children and her own mental well-being.

The divorce was not just emotionally draining - it was dangerous. Linda recounted a harrowing moment when her ex-husband, in a fit of rage, put a gun to her face.

"It was terrifying," she said, her voice steady but the weight of the memory palpable. This incident was a stark reminder of the toxicity and fear that had permeated her marriage.

The custody battle that ensued added another layer of anguish. Linda lost custody of her two sons; a pain she described as unbearable. "It felt like a part of me had been ripped away," she shared. Separated from her children and struggling to make ends meet, Linda faced financial hardships that only deepened her sense of hopelessness. "I had no choice but to keep moving forward, but there were times when I didn't think I could."

Amid the despair, Linda sought refuge in her faith and the small support system she had. Moving back to Connecticut, she stayed with her mother and began to piece her life back together. "I was angry and frustrated," she admitted, describing the emotional aftermath of her experiences. But it was this openness to her emotions, however raw and painful, that eventually paved the way for healing.

Linda's turning point came when she made the courageous decision to seek therapy. Working with the Department of Youth Services, she not only addressed her own pain but also sought help for her children. "Therapy became a lifeline," she said. "It gave me the tools to process my emotions and rebuild my relationships."

Linda's determination to reunite with her sons never wavered. Over time, she successfully regained custody, though the process was fraught with emotional and mental challenges. "Reconnecting with my boys was one of the hardest things I've ever done," she said.

Years of separation had left scars on both sides, but Linda was committed to healing those wounds.

Raising her sons as a single mother required immense bravery and strength. Linda worked multiple jobs to support them, often putting her own needs on the back burner. "I was exhausted, but I kept going," she shared.

Through sheer resilience and an openness to support, Linda slowly began to see the fruits of her efforts.

Looking back on her journey, Linda credits her survival to her desire to seek help and remain open to the process of healing. "Faith played a huge role," she said. "It gave me hope when I had none." She also emphasized the importance of community and therapy in navigating life's darkest moments.

For those facing similar challenges, Linda offers these words of wisdom:

- **Acknowledge the Pain**: "Don't bury your emotions. Let yourself feel them, but don't let them consume you."

- **Seek Support**: "You don't have to do it alone. Whether it's therapy, faith, or trusted friends, lean on the resources available to you."

- **Stay Open to Healing**: "Healing isn't linear. Be patient with yourself and trust the process."

- **Fight for What Matters**: "Even when it feels impossible, keep fighting for what's important to you. The struggle is worth it."

Today, Linda's life is a testament to the power of perseverance and faith. Though her journey was fraught with challenges, she emerged stronger and more determined to live a life rooted in openness and resilience. "I'm proud of how far I've come," she said. "The wilderness season was painful, but it taught me lessons I'll carry forever."

Her story reminds us that even in the face of profound loss and hardship, there is hope. By embracing vulnerability, seeking help, and staying open to healing, it's possible to move through the wilderness and into a life of purpose and peace.

COMPASS FRAMEWORK

MINDSET

11
FORGIVENESS

"Come to me, all you who are weary and burdened, and I will give you rest."
—Matthew 11:28 (NIV)

Forgiveness is one of the most challenging yet liberating parts of healing. For me, it wasn't a concept that came naturally. It was something I had to wrestle with, fight through, and ultimately embrace. This chapter isn't just about forgiving others; it's also about forgiving ourselves and releasing the grip that bitterness can have on our hearts and lives.

I've lived through moments where forgiveness felt impossible. One of the hardest was being abandoned by my son's father while pregnant. I was left to raise my first child alone.

Another was discovering that the person who vowed to be my partner for life had betrayed me in ways I couldn't have imagined. The pain was visceral. It wrapped itself around every corner of my mind and body. There were nights I would ruminate on the injustice, replaying conversations, rehashing the hurt, and wondering how I could ever move forward. Then came the bitterness, a poison that seeped into every part of my life. It made me feel physically ill, weighed down, and unable to see beyond the pain.

There were days when I would scroll through old text messages on a phone I had kept from that time, re-reading the words exchanged between me, my ex-husband, and someone I had once trusted. Each time I did, it was like reopening a wound and pressing into it on purpose. I knew it would hurt, but I didn't know how to stop.

I wasn't just hurting myself. I was reliving the pain, feeding it, and giving it permission to fester. It caused unhealthy thoughts to follow. It took me a long time to realize that by holding onto that bitterness, I was allowing their actions to control my life long after they had occurred.

God put it on my heart to talk about forgiveness first in this chapter because it's not just a step in healing and mindset. It's the foundation. Forgiveness doesn't excuse the actions of those who hurt us, nor does it mean reconciling with those who caused harm. Forgiveness is about release.

It is about choosing to no longer let their actions define our story or control our emotions. If we fail to forgive, we stunt progress moving forward. It's a bitter root and it's why I am addressing it head on.

One of the hardest people I ever had to forgive was the woman involved in the infidelity that led to my divorce. She admitted it to me directly, saying, "I know. I'm a homewrecker, and I can't believe I did what I did. I don't expect you to forgive me, but I hope you can."

In that moment, forgiveness felt impossible. I couldn't fathom letting go of the anger, betrayal, and pain her actions had caused. I wasn't ready, and I told her so.

But God worked on me. Over time, I began to see her not as the sum of her choices but as a broken person acting out of her own pain. I also began to hate the weight I was carrying. Holding on to unforgiveness was draining. I realized I was letting her actions live rent-free in my head, and I wanted it to end.

Less than a year later, I sent her a message letting her know I forgave her. It was not about rekindling any kind of connection. It was about releasing the hold her choices had over my life.

That act of forgiveness lifted a weight I hadn't even realized I was still carrying. Other than writing this book, she hasn't crossed my mind once since. I feel no negativity in my heart because I am no longer carrying something that does not belong to me. I could have chosen revenge or resentment, but that is God's battle, not mine.

Forgiving her opened the door for me to forgive others who had hurt me, particularly my son's father, who abandoned me during my pregnancy, long before my marriage to my daughters' father.

For years, the pain and bitterness of his absence colored my view of men and relationships. Yet, as I released my anger toward her, I discovered I could also begin to let go of my resentment toward him. And the ripple effect of forgiveness didn't stop there. I forgave my parents for mistakes that had once felt unforgivable. I forgave myself for the ways I had let my pain manifest in words and actions that didn't reflect the person I wanted to be. I also forgave myself for times I fell short as a wife, mother, friend or family member to others I cared about. For not showing up for myself or my kids in ways I knew I should have. Each act of forgiveness cleared more space in my heart and mind for growth, peace, and healing.

In moments when forgiveness felt impossible, I thought about Jesus. He didn't just talk about forgiveness;

He lived it in the most excruciating way possible. Even while dying on the cross, He said, "Father, forgive them, for they know not what they do." If Jesus could forgive in the middle of unimaginable pain, who was I to hold onto my own anger?

Forgiveness doesn't mean forgetting or pretending the hurt didn't happen. It means choosing to no longer let that pain have power over your life. It's about refusing to replay the tapes of the past that drag you down into a pit of anger and grief. For this reason, I was finally able to forgive my ex-husband. I don't know whether he, or anyone else I've chosen to forgive, has worked through their own faith or forgiveness journey, but I sincerely pray they have.

Healthy forgiveness also involves protecting your peace. Sometimes, when someone is still carrying unresolved pain, it becomes evident through the energy they bring into a room. That energy doesn't just affect them; it can shift the entire atmosphere.

After attending a recent event, my children and I felt this clearly following an interaction with someone who wasn't emotionally healthy. The heaviness lingered long after that person had left our presence. In the days that followed, two of my kids experienced panic attacks.

It was a powerful reminder that forgiveness and boundaries are both essential acts of self-respect. Forgiving someone doesn't require you to invite them back into your life or personal space. Instead, forgiveness means releasing the emotional grip they once had over you, while also honoring your right to peace and safety.

We don't talk enough about the discomfort we feel in our bodies when we're around someone who has caused us pain. And how it's *okay* to listen to that discomfort. It's not bitterness or holding a grudge, it's wisdom. It's knowing that protecting your energy is just as important as protecting your heart.

Forgiveness of self is just as important. I've had to forgive myself for the times I've hurt others, whether intentionally or not. We all carry the weight of mistakes we've made, but holding onto guilt can be as toxic as holding onto anger. I desperately pray for people who torture themselves in this way, as they don't realize that the effects of their guilt spill over onto the precious hearts of those who love them.

Forgiving others and ourselves is not just an act of grace. It's an act of power. When we let go of the bitterness and choose forgiveness, we reclaim our story. We refuse to let someone else's actions define our path. Forgiveness doesn't excuse what was done to you, but it does free you to move forward.

Practical Steps Toward Forgiveness

1. Reflect in Prayer: Ask God for help in releasing the pain and bitterness you're holding onto. Let Him guide your heart toward forgiveness.

2. Journal Your Emotions: Write down who or what you need to forgive and why. Be honest about how the pain has affected you and what you're ready to release.

3. Set Boundaries: Forgiveness doesn't mean allowing toxic people back into your life without limits. Protect your peace while letting go of resentment.

4. Speak Forgiveness Out Loud: Whether it's to the person or in private, saying the words "I forgive you" can be incredibly powerful.

5. Forgive Yourself: Reflect on areas where you've fallen short and release the guilt. Allow yourself to grow from those experiences.

A Prayer for Forgiveness

Father, help me to release the pain and anger I've been carrying. Teach me to forgive as You forgive, with grace and love. Heal the wounds in my heart and help me to move forward in peace. Guide me to let go of resentment and create space for joy and healing. Amen.

Forgiveness is one of the most courageous acts we can take. It's not easy, and it's rarely instant. But it's one of the most freeing steps in reclaiming your life and stepping into the person God created you to be. Let it go, not for them, but for you.

Reina's Journey: The Girl I Had to Forgive

Reina's journey began in a dysfunctional, very traditional, and overprotected environment. Raised in a strict Catholic household in Panama, her family upheld many customs that instilled a deep sense of guilt and shame in her from a young age. "I carried those feelings for many years," she recalled. She sought validation in the wrong places, and at sixteen, became pregnant the first time she was intimate with a man.

"Imagine this child: an A student, very overprotected, and growing up in a strict Catholic household is suddenly pregnant. It was chaos. I refused to have an abortion, and after much thought, my mom decided I should get married. As a kid, I didn't know that was an option. The decision was traumatic for me, even though I thought I was in love with the man who, unknowingly to me at the time, had taken advantage of me."

After marrying the father of her child, she hoped to create a stable family. But stability was fleeting. She gave birth to her first child, and soon after, she became pregnant again. Shortly after, her husband's abandonment left her struggling to provide for them alone.

"By the age of 20 I was homeless and desperate." She and her children found shelter in an abandoned building. "It was like living in another world. The way I needed to do laundry, the way I needed to feed my babies, to get clothing and toiletries, especially feminine products, everything was different." The irony was bitter. Her ex-husband's father was renovating the very space where she and her children hid, their lives hanging in the balance. Hunger and fear were constant companions. In a desperate attempt to survive, she made a decision she never imagined: she became a stripper.

"I told myself I needed money and that this was the easiest way. That was the lowest point in my life." The weight of this choice bore heavily on her, forcing her to live a life of secrecy. She worked in fear that the world she created to protect her children might shatter at any moment.

One night, in the dim light of that abandoned space, she looked at her children. "I felt as if I was out of my body. The smell of sawdust in the dimly lit room, the echoes of violence throughout the city, and my baby's sweet voice while playing on the mattress created such cognitive dissonance in my mind and pain in my heart. My boys didn't belong there, and it was up to me to get them out of that environment. Something snapped. Everything crashed down." The thought of losing them- of giving up her youngest child to a European woman who had offered to adopt, was unbearable.

Reina recalls, "She told me she could help me, help my kids. She couldn't have children and wanted to take my youngest. That terrified me. That was the moment I knew I had to end this." That terror fueled her determination.

She sought knowledge, devouring books, trying to understand how to break free from the chains of her circumstances. "I read the books, watched the videos, and did everything the gurus said would work, but it wasn't working for me." But knowledge alone wasn't enough. "I kept thinking, 'I have to do this for my boys.' I tried to go back to the girl I used to be, but she was gone."

The patterns of survival had been ingrained in her for so long that change felt impossible. Depression took hold, and thoughts of ending it all crept in. Yet, each time, her children's faces reminded her of her reason to fight.

Faith, once a cornerstone of her upbringing, she now felt distant. She wasn't the same person she once was, and she wasn't sure how to reconnect with the beliefs she had left behind. "I thought God had forgotten about me." The trauma had altered her, physically and mentally. "I believed something in my brain had changed permanently, that I was damaged beyond repair." Deep down, she knew she wasn't the only one who had suffered through such a journey. Perhaps sharing her story could help someone else find their way.

Despite the fear, Reina found moments of resilience. She built small habits to move forward, even when it felt impossible. She sought jobs that offered stability, even if they paid little. She found solace in tiny victories like buying a meal for her children, securing temporary housing or reading a new book that inspired her. Each step felt insurmountable at first, "Even after we moved out of that building, I remained mentally in that dimly lit room for a while," but she kept going.

Reina also learned to change her mindset. "I realized my past shaped me, but it didn't have to define my future." She focused on the lessons she could take from her struggles rather than being consumed by them. She reframed her thoughts, teaching herself to see possibilities rather than barriers. Instead of dwelling on her mistakes, she asked herself what she could do differently moving forward.

She surrounded herself with people who uplifted her, distancing herself from toxic environments that reinforced her old ways of thinking. She discovered that healing wasn't just about changing circumstances, it was about changing how she viewed herself and her worth. Her determination to rewrite her story became stronger than her fear of failing.

Through sheer resilience and a shift in mindset, Reina transformed her life. She found work, established a sense of stability, and reconnected with her faith in a way that was meaningful to her. She built a foundation for her children, determined to provide them with opportunities she never had. "The past was still with me, but I was no longer trapped by it. My journey is still unfolding, but I've already come so far."

Today, Reina uses the hard-earned wisdom from her journey to help others find their way. She now works as a financial coach, guiding individuals to break free from limiting money beliefs and create lives aligned with their values. Through her work, she's found healing in helping others rewrite their own stories - just as she continues to rewrite hers.

12
GETTING UNSTUCK

"Do not conform to the pattern of this world, but be transformed by the renewing of your mind. Then you will be able to test and approve what God's will is-His good, pleasing and perfect will."
Romans 12:2 NIV

Feeling stuck sucks. You wake up knowing something must change, but you have no idea where to even start. Been there, done that, bought the T-shirt. It's like standing at the edge of a forest with no map, no compass, and no clue which direction leads to daylight. But here's the good news: you don't have to stay stuck.

I know because I've been there. After my divorce, I spent plenty of days feeling like I was going in circles, waiting for some magical answer to appear. Spoiler: the magic doesn't come until *you* take the first step. But once you do? That's when the good stuff happens.

Ask yourself this question. Am I ready for the good part? Then smile even if your face doesn't feel like doing it. Did you know your face muscles will trick your brain into thinking you're feeling positive or even happy even if you fake a smile? It's all part of shifting our energy.

Let's keep going.

When life feels like a mess, grounding yourself is step one. Think of it as hitting "pause" on all the noise in your head. A simple grounding exercise can help. Right now, wherever you are, take a deep breath with me.

Inhale for four seconds. Hold it for four. Now exhale for four and hold again for four. Do it again.

Now, look around. Name three things you see. Maybe it's the couch, your coffee cup, or even your dog snoring in the corner. That's it- you're in the moment. It's not complicated, but it's powerful because it disrupts the pattern.

Here's another strategy I use: Gratitude. Yep. Feeling grateful and not just saying I'm thankful.

And I'm not talking about pretending everything is fine when it's not. Gratitude is about finding *something*, literally *anything* you can appreciate in this moment. For me, on the hardest days, it was as small as, "I'm grateful my coffee is hot." or "I'm grateful I had hot water for my shower" or even, "I'm grateful I felt a little less sad today than I did yesterday".

Start there.

When you're stuck, even thinking about a plan feels overwhelming. So don't think about the *whole* plan. Just think about the next step.

Here's What Helped Me:

1. **Pick One Thing**. You don't have to solve your entire life today. Pick one area to focus on, whether it's your emotions, your finances or your health, whatever feels doable.

2. **Set a Small Goal**. Forget big, fancy goals for now. Just think about what you can do *this week*. Maybe it's drinking an extra glass of water each day or spending 10 minutes journaling. For me, it was walking a little each morning for one week.

3. **Write It Down**. Grab a notebook or open your notes

app. Writing it down makes it feel real and crossing it off or checking a box later feels amazing.

Don't overthink this. **Progress, not perfection,** is the goal. That became my mantra for the entire journey of my healing.

There were so many days I didn't feel strong enough to move forward. That's when I leaned on other people's stories. Seeing others who had been through the same wilderness gave me hope.

If you're in a space where you don't feel confident, borrow it. Borrow it from me. Borrow it from the stories in this book, your friends, or someone in your group. You don't have to have it all figured out right now. Just trust that if others have found a way, you can too.

Here are a few simple ways to shake things up and get unstuck:

- Move your Body. Go for a walk, take a shower, do some stretches, or have a solo dance party in your kitchen. Movement changes your energy. Go shake what your mama gave ya!

- Join the Conversation. Connect with others who get it. If you're in a group, jump in. Comment on posts, ask questions, share what's on your mind.

Sometimes the smallest actions make the biggest difference.

So, what's your next step? **Show up for yourself!**

Here's your challenge:

What's one thing you can do today to show up for yourself? Maybe it's getting outside for fresh air, texting a friend, or writing down a single goal. Whatever it is, *do it*.

And remember, you do not have to do this alone. I am here cheering you on, and there is a growing circle of women who are healing, growing, and rediscovering who they are.

If you are ready to go deeper, stay connected through updates at wildernesswisdombook.com. You will find more tools, workshops, and ways to support your journey.

You've got this. One small step at a time, you are moving forward. And soon, you will look back and see that you were not stuck. You were becoming. Keep going.

Even in seasons of wilderness, there comes a time when you have to look toward the future if you want to move forward. And that shift has a lot to do with being actively involved in your own journey. You might find yourself thinking, "Okay, I'm stuck here right now. I don't know where this is going." But the truth is, when you start to feel better, you'll begin to do better.

Reframing the way you think about your circumstances, your emotions, and even your physical symptoms can be transformative. Emotional thoughts and self-talk don't just affect your mood; they influence your brain and your body's ability to heal. Our thoughts are powerful. When we begin to rewire how we think, we take back control of our healing process.

Once I grasped hold of this principle, I began to heal dramatically. I changed my diet, lost over 60 pounds, and embraced a completely new mindset. It wasn't just about physical changes, it really wasn't! It was about letting go of limiting beliefs and taking ownership of my healing. I began to understand that symptoms are not just problems to be solved but messages from our bodies, guiding us toward balance and wellness.

During my separation and after my divorce, my therapy sessions helped me identify what I needed for my healing. One of the most important exercises was writing down boundaries. What I needed to do to take ownership of protecting my emotional well-being in order to move forward. I realized that I couldn't continue to be a constant source of support for others or believe promises and intentions without evidence or action. These notes became a blueprint for creating space for my own healing and growth.

Practical Tools:

Healing requires a holistic approach. Here are some tools I've found invaluable on the journey:

- Reframe your self-talk: Instead of identifying with a diagnosis, say, "I am healing from _____."
- Release repressed emotions and focus on increasing positive emotions.
- Change your surroundings to promote healing.
- Ground yourself and deepen your spiritual connection.
- Have strong reasons for living and embrace social support.

I am very interested in the psychology of healing and disease. Your surroundings affect your healing. When I moved to South Carolina from New Jersey, I noticed my environment affected my healing just as much as the people on my journey did. Seeing the sunshine, spending time at the ocean. Meeting new people who also were new to the area and wanted to make friendships. Being closer to my family who live here. A positive and uplifting church. It all helped.

Limiting beliefs can block your healing. The way we

think about our symptoms and challenges matters more than we realize. Sometimes, symptoms are simply your body's way of asking for support and signaling that healing is needed. Instead of letting them steal your joy or derail your day, choose to be present. You can still enjoy life in the midst of your healing journey.

Grounding practices, shifting your mindset, and making intentional changes can help move you forward. This includes things like changing your diet, using natural support like herbs and supplements, and deepening your spiritual connection. Trust your intuition, or as I like to say, the nudge of the Holy Spirit. Releasing repressed emotions, increasing positive emotions, and embracing social support are also key to recovery. Having strong reasons for living fuels your motivation to keep going.

I'm a recovering perfectionist. I worked through a lot in therapy. I remember journaling things like:

- Write out the boundaries I need others to respect in order for me to heal.

- Talk about why I cannot be someone else's constant source of support.

- Pay attention to whether someone's actions match their words, including my own.

- Ask myself why it still hurts so deeply when others seem to move on so quickly.

- Acknowledge that I will never be able to fully understand why betrayal happens but that I can only control how I heal moving forward.

- Consider whether it would be healthier if I lived elsewhere for a while.

- Recognize that without proof of change, it's just words

and empty promises.

That season taught me that **mindset matters**. Shifting your perspective is one of the most powerful ways to get unstuck. Ask yourself the hard questions. Start small. Reflect on what limiting beliefs may still be holding you back. What boundaries are missing that could protect your peace?

The Bible reminds us to renew our minds:

"Do not conform to the pattern of this world, but be transformed by the renewing of your mind. Then you will be able to test and approve what God's will is—his good, pleasing and perfect will."

— Romans 12:2 (NIV)

Creating simple daily habits can strengthen your mental and spiritual health. Practices like journaling, prayer, walking, and grounding help release emotional weight and bring clarity. The connection between physical wellness and mental fitness is real.

One of the tools that helped me shift my mindset and regain a sense of control during my healing process is the **MIRACLE Morning S.A.V.E.R.S. routine** by Hal Elrod. It's a simple yet powerful morning practice that sets the tone for the day with intention and clarity. Each letter in the acronym represents a different element of personal growth and mental fitness:

• **Silence**

Starting the day with stillness creates space to hear yourself and hear from God. Whether it's prayer, breathwork, or quiet reflection, this moment of silence helps you feel grounded before the noise of the world can get in.

- **Affirmations**

These are intentional, truth-based statements that remind you of who you are and where you are going. Speaking affirmations daily helps retrain your thoughts and build a stronger, more empowered mindset. It's not about pretending everything is perfect. It's about calling in what you are actively working toward.

- **Visualization**

This is where you take a moment to see the version of yourself you are becoming. Picture yourself healed, thriving, and at peace. Visualization builds motivation and gives your mind a clear image to move toward, especially on days when you feel stuck or overwhelmed.

- **Exercise**

You don't need an hour-long gym session. A short walk, stretching, or dancing in your kitchen can be enough to activate your energy and support emotional regulation. Movement reminds your body that you are still in control and taking steps forward.

- **Reading**

Even just a few pages of something uplifting or wisdom-filled can shift your mindset. This is where growth happens through learning. Whether it's scripture, personal development, or stories of others who have overcome, reading feeds your soul and helps expand your thinking.

- **Scribing (Journaling)**

Writing things down can be one of the most healing practices of all. It allows you to release what's on your mind, track your growth, and capture both the wins and the struggles. Some days it might be a gratitude list. Other days it's simply letting your emotions spill onto the page. Either way, journaling supports clarity and healing.

I didn't master these habits overnight, and some mornings were messy or missed entirely. But when I showed up, I felt the difference. Starting the day with intention helps me stay grounded, even in the middle of chaos.

Healing isn't about perfection or having all the answers. It's about taking small, honest steps forward. When we shift our mindset, release what no longer serves us, and choose to show up with grace, we create space for joy, clarity, and transformation.

Steps to Strengthen Your Mindset:

1. **Affirm Your Identity:** Write down who you are and what you stand for. Repeat it to yourself daily.

2. **Shift Your Focus:** Release the things you can't fix and focus on one small step you can take today.

3. **Create Space for Stillness:** Spend a few moments each day in quiet reflection or prayer to center your heart and mind.

Amanda's Story:
Trusting the Voice Within

This is the story of a woman who learned that No is a holy word. And that standing firm isn't defiance - it's obedience.

"I knew he was drinking more, but I didn't realize how bad it had gotten, until I twisted open a bottled beer one night and took a sip. It was water. That's when I realized he was hiding it, replacing bottles with water to cover how much he was drinking."

Amanda's voice cracked a little as she shared that moment. It was just one scene in a much bigger, messier unraveling she couldn't see coming. At the time, she had no idea how deep it would actually go.

Just two weeks after their first child was born, Amanda and her husband were already sitting in counseling, trying to figure out what was happening. But she could feel the lies tightening around her like a net. "I didn't understand boundaries. I thought I was supposed to love, forgive, and turn the other cheek. That's what the church taught me. That's what I thought God wanted."

Years of emotional erosion followed. Her husband never admitted to having a problem. The drinking escalated into drugs, then stealing, then prostitution.

By the time their youngest son was a toddler, things had deteriorated significantly. Her husband lashed out at her parents and became increasingly unsafe around the children. "He didn't bar-hop or stumble around drunk in public. It was always at night, behind closed doors. But when it started happening during the day and around the kids, I was done." ▽116

She asked him to leave, thinking that would be the hardest part. But it wasn't. "When you're still in the house together, you can monitor things. You can control the environment a little. But once you leave that and try to protect your kids from afar, the real nightmare begins."

What followed were years of courtrooms, custody mediations, and betrayal. Amanda hired an attorney, but still found herself manipulated by a system that didn't believe her. "And then came the games. DSS calls. Accusations. Gaslighting. And the attorneys? They didn't want truth, they wanted closure."

Amanda's middle son became ammunition in the custody battle. Her ex used him to emotionally manipulate the situation, creating wedges between them. Eventually, Amanda made a heart-wrenching decision. "I had to surrender. I had no power to parent the way I needed to. He went to live with his dad. It was a very dark time, and I felt hopeless."

But then came the moment Amanda calls the real wilderness. It was the night before their son's 15th birthday. He had been living with his father.

"They went into town. His dad had been drinking all day. Our son asked him to stay in the car because he was embarrassed. That set him off. My ex was explosive the entire ride, and when they returned home, he said to our son, 'You're the reason my life is like this. Let's just end it.' Then he went inside, got his gun, and chased our son across the backyard. And he fired."

Amanda's voice cracked. "My son ran into the woods and hid. He debated calling the police for over an hour because he was afraid they'd shoot his father. But he finally called."

Amanda only found out because his phone was still on her plan. She saw the 911 alert. When she called, he answered sobbing: "I'm sorry, Mom. I'm sorry."

Despite all this, the court still allowed her ex-husband visitation. "He had every drug in his system at mediation. And they still said he could have rights as long as he didn't use around the kids."

Amanda was urged by her attorney, the guardian ad litem, and the mediator to settle. They wanted her to agree to supervised visits being dropped, to stop drug tests, to accept unpaid medical bills from trauma therapy for the children.

But Amanda had changed. She had started spending time with God every single day. Reading Scripture, praying, listening. "I dropped to my knees and asked the Lord what to do. And I heard Him say, 'Stand firm.'"

It was the first time she ever said No and meant it. She told everyone involved: No. She would not settle. She would not drop her demands. She would not betray her children's safety again.

Her attorney pushed hard. There were days of back-and-forth emails, phone calls, and mounting pressure. Amanda could feel the heat rising every time she refused. "She was frustrated with me," Amanda recalls. "I could tell she thought I was being stubborn or unrealistic." But Amanda wasn't just responding from emotion anymore. She was listening to the Lord.

And then, when no one expected it, least of all her attorney, her ex agreed to everything. "I was sitting at the bus stop when my attorney texted me and said, 'I can't believe this, but he agreed to every single thing.'"

She wept. Not from fear or defeat, but from the holy shock of victory.

Even now, she sometimes wonders if she overreacted. If maybe, like he said, she was being dramatic. "But God saw what no one else did. And He told me to stand. So I did."

In the end, she hadn't overreacted at all. The very thing she had tried to protect her children from, the addiction he insisted didn't exist, was real. Less than a year later, he overdosed and lost his life.

And though devastating, it confirmed what the Spirit had been whispering all along: They weren't safe in his care. Her "No" wasn't just a boundary. It was a rescue mission. God used her obedience to shield her children from a reality too dangerous to ignore.

The system wasn't built to protect her or her children. The church hadn't prepared her. The people she trusted had failed. But the Holy Spirit had not.

Amanda now knows that trusting your gut is often the Holy Spirit speaking. "Your body knows. Your soul knows."

She's learned that boundaries are biblical. That fleeing from wickedness is scriptural. And that trusting God isn't passive - it's a bold act of resistance!

"If I had gone to Him sooner, I wonder if we would have suffered so much? But I thought loving meant sacrificing everything. That's not what God wanted for me or my kids."

Amanda's journey through spiritual abuse, legal

injustice, and maternal heartbreak didn't destroy her. It awakened her. She hopes to teach others how to recognize toxicity, trust God's voice, and guard their hearts without guilt.

"I allowed it. That's the hardest part to admit. But it also means I can learn. I can grow. I can break the cycle."

Her wilderness journey wasn't just about escaping danger. It was about reclaiming discernment. It was about remembering who she was - and Whose Daughter she is.

Amanda is no longer silent. And she wants every woman reading this to know:

"You are not crazy. You are not alone. And your 'No' can be the start of everything new."

"When I look back now, I can see God's hand in all of it," Amanda reflected. "Even in the worst moments, He was preparing me for something better."

Amanda's story reminds us that no wilderness lasts forever. You may feel stuck right now, but each step forward - no matter how small, moves you closer to the light. Stand firm. Trust God's compass. The wilderness may shape you, but it will never define you.

Lessons from Amanda's Journey

1. **Mindset Shapes the Path:** Your thoughts determine your direction. Choose to trust in your strength and God's plan.

2. **Faith Anchors You:** Even when everything feels impossible, trust that God is fighting for you.

3. **Self-Care is Essential:** Protect your peace so you have the strength to keep moving forward.

Reflection Prompt:

- Have you ignored your gut or God's voice because others convinced you not to trust yourself?

- What do you need to say "No" to in your life today?

- What would it mean to believe God is fighting for you right now?

Journal It:

- What are some situations where you felt God speaking but you ignored it? What happened?

- Write down one area where you want to build stronger boundaries.

- What scripture speaks to your need for discernment or protection right now?

- What would it look like for you to fully trust the Holy Spirit, even when the world says otherwise?

COMPASS FRAMEWORK

PURPOSEFUL
MOVEMENT

13
MOVEMENT & MOTIVATION

"She is clothed with strength and dignity; she laughs without fear of the future." Proverbs 31:25

In her devotional, Promises for Our Everyday Lives, Joyce Meyer states that "We have to conquer the wilderness mentality."

She points out that the Israelites wandered around the wilderness for forty years to make what was actually an eleven-day journey. Why did they do this? Her revelation was: "The Israelites couldn't move on because they had a wilderness mentality." The Israelites had no positive vision for their lives, no dreams. They needed to let go of that mentality and trust God.

Much like the Israelites in this scenario, we too can also get stuck in a loop. Ruminate on the same thing over and over again until we walk around our own "mountain" of wilderness instead of making progress to move forward from it. Why does it take us so long to slay these giants? But once we finally do, we realize we could have done that thing years ago because it wasn't so bad. What kind of time could we have saved had we dealt with it and moved on, leaving it in the past, where it belongs?

The Bible speaks about the importance of renewing our minds and how it shapes our faith and ability to embrace change. Establishing a new mindset is essential, it empowers us to believe that transformation is possible and opens the door for us to partner with God as He reveals the steps to move forward. As Deuteronomy 1:6 reminds us, "The Lord our God said to us at Horeb, 'You have stayed long enough at this mountain.'" It's a call to stop dwelling in stagnation and take action toward what's next.

Taking God's word and putting it into action has always started well for me, but sticking with it and following through has continuously been a challenge. I knew I needed to research the best ways to help myself not just believe I could do it, but visualize myself doing it when it felt hard, got boring or if the outcome wasn't coming fast enough for me. Ever get impatient? Yeah, that's another of my character traits. I like things to move along quickly when I know what I want and when they don't, boy does it irk me.

One of the most pivotal moments in my journey was choosing to stop standing still. I made the decision to invest in my healing and rediscover who I was beyond the heartbreak. I didn't have a roadmap, but I quickly learned that clarity often comes after you take action. Just one small step was enough to start moving forward. I leaned into resources like books, podcasts, coaching, and therapy, and surrounded myself with people who had walked similar paths and could offer real guidance.

Rebuilding wasn't just about regaining financial footing. It was about healing the emotional wounds left behind and reclaiming my sense of identity. One of the boldest steps I took was changing my name, marking a fresh start and a new chapter. It wasn't easy. As I've shared before, I lost friendships, had to reconnect with myself, and face the fear of vulnerability. But I knew isolation would only stall my growth, so I kept showing up, attending events, building new connections, and staying committed to the process.

To create stability, I temporarily returned to a traditional W2 job. It gave me breathing room while I focused on building healthier habits in my personal life. Walking, grounding, and consistent movement became part of my daily routine. These practices reminded me that even small steps, when taken consistently, can lead to real transformation. Letting go of alcohol and recommitting to my physical health were major turning points. They didn't just improve my energy and clarity. They helped me believe in my ability to build something better.

Over time, walking became more than just a daily habit. It became a gateway. Once I stopped dreading movement and started enjoying how I felt afterward, I leaned all the way in. I started cleaning up my diet, not perfectly, but intentionally. I traded stress-snacking and takeout for meals that supported my health and didn't leave me feeling sluggish. From there, I explored different types of exercise. Some days it was cardio or jogging. Other days I was lifting weights or doing HIIT workouts that made me question every life decision that led me to join the online fitness program I belonged to. I ran in three 5Ks and started hiking regularly. There were sore muscles, awkward stretches, and the occasional moment of rage during push-ups, but I kept showing up, and it changed everything.

Two of my most memorable milestones were ziplining in the mountains of North Carolina and tackling a challenging hike in Hawaii. The ziplining experience was one for the books. I had one of those *"What was I thinking?"* moments as soon as I reached the platform. My heart was pounding, my palms were sweaty, and my legs were having a full-on protest. Just as panic started to rise, my son looked over, saw it all in my face, and calmly said, "I'll go first, Mom. Just follow me." Then he jumped without hesitation. Like a total boss. And there I was, a grown woman, being shown up by my own child. I screamed most of the way, but I did it. I didn't die, and more importantly, I didn't let fear win.

That moment stuck with me. If I had stayed still, both physically and mentally, I would have missed it. That hike in Hawaii? Same thing. It was steep, sweaty, and full of inner complaints like, "this better be worth it." But at the top, the view stopped me in my tracks. I had made it through something hard, again. That's what movement does. It reminds you of what you're capable of. You don't need to start big. Just start. Each choice to move forward adds up, and one day, you realize you're living a life you never thought you'd be strong enough to build. Possibly screaming through the air, but fully alive.

1. What small, intentional actions can you take today to move closer to the life you envision?

2. Who or what can you lean on for support and encouragement when the journey feels overwhelming?

3. How can you cultivate resilience in your daily routines to stay grounded and focused, even during life's toughest seasons?

14

MOVING WITH PURPOSE

BY MICHELLE GRIFFIN

The agony of living in my house was unbearable. I had done everything I could to be a great wife, an attentive mother, a hard worker, and a good friend. But no matter how much I gave, it was never enough. The home I had worked so hard to create had become a prison. The energy in that space was suffocating, a constant reminder of everything that was broken.

It didn't matter how much I cleaned, how many meals I cooked, how many practices I took our boys to, how much money I made, or how much of myself I gave away. The head of our household was miserable, and that misery seeped into every corner of our lives. I had three sons who didn't respect me because their father had shown them, by example, that I wasn't worthy of respect.

I had tried to leave before. But every time I expressed my unhappiness, my husband would "change" just long enough to convince me to sign another lease, to renew the commitment I already knew was draining me. It went on like that for years. Sixteen years of believing in something that wasn't real, hoping for a transformation that was never going to come. I finally realized that he never wanted to change, he only wanted the illusion of a happy home as long as it didn't require any real effort on his part.

To keep my sanity, I needed refuge. God had always

been my ultimate refuge, but I needed a physical space where I could breathe, where I could feel safe, where I could create a new reality. That opportunity came in an unexpected way.

One night, my middle son misbehaved, and his father took every electronic device (TV, gaming system, phone) out of his room as punishment. My son, not wanting to sleep in an empty room, moved to the couch. And just like that, an idea sparked. That empty room? It became mine.

I didn't need a TV or distractions. I just needed space. I needed a door that I could close between myself and the negativity that had consumed my life. For the first time in years, I had a room of my own, a place where I could begin reclaiming my peace. That small shift changed everything. It wasn't just about sleeping in a different room, it was the decision to separate myself from the toxicity, to take control of my environment, to start seeing myself as an individual again. From that moment on, I functioned as if I didn't live in the house. I mentally detached, making decisions for myself and my children without factoring in my husband's influence. That separation was the first step toward real freedom.

Then, a miracle happened. A dear friend of mine had a father who needed care in another part of the country. She had watched me struggle in my marriage for years, and she knew I was desperate for a way out. So, when she decided to move, she offered to rent her three-bedroom home to me at an affordable price—a place where I could finally have a fresh start as a single mom.

This wasn't a coincidence. It was a *Godincidence*.

That home became my sanctuary, a place where I could finally exhale. After years of feeling confined, verbally attacked, and mentally exhausted, I was stepping into a new life—not just for myself, but for my children. We were creating something new, something healthy. This was our chance to rewrite our story.

Through it all, my faith never wavered. Even in the darkest moments, I knew God had a plan for me. The confirmations came in waves, blessings I couldn't ignore, reminders that I was exactly where I needed to be. The home He provided became more than just a refuge for me and my boys. During the pandemic, it was also a safe place for my sister and her children. It was a space filled with love and restoration.

During that time, I started recording a podcast called *Strength in the Moment*. I had been given so much strength during my journey, and I knew it was my responsibility to share it with others who were struggling. My life was no longer just about surviving, I was stepping into my purpose, into the life God had intended for me all along.

One of the most important lessons I learned through this experience is the power of your environment. The spaces we occupy and the people we surround ourselves with shape our reality. I began to realize that *my* happy place could be anywhere I chose, if I was intentional about the energy I allowed into my life.

If something didn't sit right in my spirit, I had the power to walk away. Whether it was a toxic person, a draining job, or an unhealthy mindset, I didn't have to stay stuck. I could make a different choice. I could *move*. That realization was life changing. I had spent so long believing I was trapped, but the truth was, I had control all along.

I had control over my **thoughts**. I could choose to see the glass as half empty, half full, or simply be grateful I had a glass at all.

I had control over my **inner circle**. I could surround myself with people who poured into me rather than drained me.

I had control over my **incoming information**. I didn't have to fill my mind with negativity from the news or toxic social media. I could choose peace.

I had control over my **decisions**. Every single choice, big or small, was an opportunity to shape my future.

And I had control over my **perspective**. I could focus on the hardships, or I could focus on the blessings. No matter what, I always had a choice.

Looking back, I see now that my transformation wasn't just about leaving my marriage. It was about reclaiming my power. It was about realizing that I wasn't stuck, that I had the authority to create the life I wanted. Change doesn't happen by accident. It happens when we make *intentional* choices to move forward, even when it's hard, even when we're scared.

I encourage you to examine your own life. What environments are you choosing to stay in that no longer serve you? Who are you allowing into your space? What thoughts are you entertaining that are holding you back?

When you start to shift these things, when you move with purpose, everything changes. Never underestimate the power of your perspective. Never underestimate the power of *your* choices. You are stronger than you think, and you are fully capable of creating the life God intended for you.

15

I AM A BADASS

BY SONJA REVELLS

I knew I was sick. I hadn't been feeling well for a while - always tired, night sweats, and constantly feeling like I was on the verge of getting the flu. Then the swelling in my neck drastically and dramatically increased. At the time, I didn't have health insurance and was waiting for open enrollment to end so that my coverage could begin. As soon as it did, I scheduled an appointment with a primary care doctor.

That appointment led to blood tests, then a CT scan, then a specialist, and then a needle biopsy, which didn't take. Finally, I had a lymph node removed.

I read the results in the online portal and **knew** - it was cancer.

A few days later, I was sitting in the doctor's office at the Levine Cancer Center in Charlotte, North Carolina. My newfound oncologist confirmed what I already suspected. What I didn't know, however, was the type of cancer I had.

I was diagnosed with Hodgkin's Lymphoma, Stage 4B. I didn't even know there was a "B" stage.

The doctor explained that I would lose my hair, need to undergo chemotherapy immediately, and would require a total of 12 rounds. Due to the severity of my condition, I would also need a port implanted just under the right side of my collarbone.

Out of all the cancers to have, Hodgkin's Lymphoma had the highest survival rate.

I cried. The doctors were kind and sympathetic as they explained my diagnosis and what to expect. But their words echoed from a distance.

Initially, I didn't want to undergo chemotherapy. I wanted to approach treatment holistically, using natural and alternative methods. However, pursuing those options required both time and money - two things I didn't have. My cancer was aggressive, and I soon developed what is called "the Hodgkin's rash."

The rash covered most of my body, making it nearly impossible to sleep. Every shower or bath felt like battery acid being poured over me.

Those sores were worse than the chemo. So, I went from not wanting chemotherapy to eagerly awaiting my first treatment.

The physical and emotional toll was immense, but the financial burden was even harder. Letting go of my ego was one of the most challenging parts of this journey. Living alone, working when I could, and going through chemo meant I eventually had to face the reality that I needed financial help. I cried a lot when I accepted this truth.

It was humbling and painful to create a GoFundMe to ask for support. With each treatment, I counted down how many rounds I had left and shared updates on my GoFundMe page and occasionally on Facebook.

For me, resilience meant driving myself 30–45 minutes to the Levine Cancer Center for each round of chemotherapy. I'd spend five to six hours there, surrounded by beeping machines and others fighting their own battles. After treatment, I'd drive myself home and walk my 100-pound dog, Mojo.

At the time, I lived in a second-floor apartment. Climbing those stairs after chemo, battling fatigue, was a challenge, but I made it a point to walk Mojo three times a day, every day. Occasionally, friends or neighbors helped on extra-tough days, but most of the time, it was just me and my boy.

I also worked out at least one day a week with a friend who was a personal trainer. I was determined not to lose all the muscle I had built in the year and a half before my diagnosis. Although I lost a lot of muscle, I lost even more fat. I'll never forget how upset I was about losing my butt more than losing my hair!

Losing my hair was one of the hardest parts. My long, beautiful hair had been part of my identity for as long as I could remember. Watching it fall out in clumps was devastating, but eventually, I shaved it off myself. Later, I got a head crown henna tattoo while attending an Indian festival in the city - a way of reclaiming a part of myself.

The support I received during this time kept me going. My family, friends, and the incredible women in my real estate investing network encouraged me every step of the way. I'll never forget one of my mentorship calls during my treatments. A woman on the call said, "Sonja is a badass!" Our coach energetically agreed, "Sonja IS a badass." At the time, I didn't see myself that way, but looking back, I realized: I am a Badass.

I leaned heavily on the Miracle Morning practice that Hal Elrod coined. His SAVERS routine -Silence,

Affirmations, Visualization, Exercise, Reading, and Scribing, became my anchor. I created a vision board with future goals, things I wanted to buy, places to visit, and ways to help family and friends. Holding those visions helped me through the roughest days and reminded me that what I was going through was temporary.

I also thought deeply about what I hadn't yet accomplished in life. If it was my time to die, what would I regret not achieving? Only two things came to mind. Those regrets became my guiding force, crystalizing where I would focus my energy once I finished chemo.

Eventually, I finished chemo. I was in remission, but I was also completely broke, further in debt, and facing eviction from my apartment. That was almost exactly one year ago.

Over the past year, I've started making strides in the two areas I want to succeed in. I've learned to better identify situations and people that cause extreme stress and how to limit my involvement with them.

The wilderness shaped me, but it didn't define me. Hopefully, I'll continue making strides and stay in remission.

Author Note: As we close this section on motivation and movement, it's important to recognize that even the smallest steps can lead to monumental transformations. True progress often begins with a decision to move forward, no matter how uncertain or challenging the path may seem. The two chapters you just read include incredible stories of overcoming a major place of pivot and purpose through resilience and determination. Take a moment to reflect on your own.

COMPASS FRAMEWORK

ACCOUNTABILITY

16

WHAT I HAD TO OWN TO GET FREE

There's a point in healing where a shift occurs. Not because everything got better, but because you finally got honest.

Honest about what you allowed.

What you avoided.

What you ignored.

What you weren't willing to face in yourself.

And that kind of honesty? It's uncomfortable.

So is change.

It stretches you, challenges what you've known, and often demands more than you think you have.

But healing won't wait for comfort.

It begins the moment you decide that staying stuck hurts more than growing ever could.

Accountability isn't about blaming yourself for what others did.

It's about taking ownership of your growth.

Of your boundaries.

Of the healing no one can do for you.

That's where freedom begins. It's where I savored my first taste of true liberation.

Accountability is such a powerful part of healing that leads to transformation, not just in walking away from pain, but in choosing not to stay stuck in it.

I remember standing in my own wilderness season, holding the pieces of a life that no longer made sense. And as easy as it would have been to keep pointing to what was done *to* me, I knew deep down: if I wanted *different*, I had to *do* different.

No one was coming to rescue me. I had to show up for my healing.

So, I started small.

Habits.

Journals.

Morning routines.

Redoing a vision board that didn't make sense at the time.

I said no to things that drained me. I set goals that scared the crap out of me. I stopped waiting to feel ready and started moving forward, even when I didn't know where I was headed. That's what **accountability** looks like in real life. It's not about shame, it's about ownership. It's about drawing a line and saying, *"The pain wasn't my fault.* ***But my healing? That's mine to claim."***

Accountability isn't a punishment. It's an invitation. It's

the moment you stop waiting for someone else to change and realize you hold the keys to your own peace.

What helped me most was creating **simple, repeatable systems** to track progress, keep momentum, and stay aligned with the version of myself I was becoming. Whether it was checking off a small daily win or reflecting on how far I'd come that week, those systems gave me structure when everything felt chaotic.

I also built a community of safe people, those who truly wanted to see me heal and grow. I shared my goals with them, asked for their support, and allowed them to lovingly check in with me. That kind of relational accountability helped me stay grounded. And yes, I also invested in a coach or three who challenged me, held space for me, and didn't let me play small. Because sometimes, accountability means letting others hold you to the standard you're reaching for.

Accountability gave me traction when nothing else did. Not perfection. Not a clear plan. Just one choice after another rooted in honesty, consistency, and the desire to write a different ending to my story.

If you've been waiting for permission to get honest with yourself and begin again... consider this it.

Before you read Elizabeth's story that illustrates this type of accountability, I want to pause and talk about a topic that comes up a lot in circles but isn't always addressed directly: narcissistic abuse.

We're hearing more about it lately, online, in support groups, in therapy sessions... and for good reason. Narcissism isn't just a buzzword. It's a pattern of behavior rooted in a deep lack of empathy, an inflated sense of self, and a need to control and manipulate. It's not always loud or explosive. Sometimes it's subtle, slow, and incredibly confusing. And it can come from anyone, not just men, not just partners. Narcissistic traits can show up in parents, siblings, bosses, and even close friends. It's not about a diagnosis - it's about the impact.

The Bible warns us about this kind of behavior:

"But understand this, that in the last days there will come times of difficulty. For people will be lovers of self, lovers of money, proud, arrogant, abusive... having the appearance of godliness, but denying its power. Avoid such people."
—2 Timothy 3:1–5

Jesus Himself called out the religious leaders of His time for their arrogance, hypocrisy, and lack of compassion. This isn't new. But what is new, for many of us, is the moment we wake up and realize we've been living in that fog for too long.

When we name narcissistic behavior for what it is, we're not labeling to shame...we're labeling to bring clarity. Because healing begins with honesty. And accountability starts with calling things what they are.

Elizabeth's story is about the moment she stopped explaining away someone else's behavior and started reclaiming her own truth. That's what accountability looks like, it's the choice to walk out of the fog and into the light. It's not just emotional clarity. It's also practical: establishing systems for self-monitoring and progress tracking. The things that keep us grounded, focused, and moving forward even when it's hard.

Accountability helps us follow through on our healing, stay aligned with our growth, and honor our vision for something better.

Elizabeth's Story
Rewriting the Map:
Breaking the Cycle for Good

The moment Elizabeth realized she was lost in a wilderness season didn't come with a thunderclap. It came on a Saturday morning, ten weeks after giving birth. Her daughter was just a few months old, and her husband had become increasingly cruel, cold, dismissive, and hateful.

"I gotta get out of this," she remembers saying. At the time, she didn't think it was permanent. She thought maybe she just needed a break. But that morning was the beginning of her escape from a toxic, narcissistic relationship that had been simmering with emotional and financial abuse for years.

Elizabeth didn't know the word *narcissist* at first. She just knew something was terribly wrong. The abuse had escalated during her pregnancy. What should have been a sacred time became a season of isolation, anxiety, and dread. Her ex's mask had slipped. Elizabeth shared that once she became pregnant, his behavior shifted dramatically, he became more withdrawn, irritable, and emotionally distant. As her pregnancy progressed, she found herself increasingly isolated, anxious, and unsure of what was real.

She later learned about terms like love bombing, gaslighting, and discarding. These are tools commonly referenced in narcissistic relationship cycles and she began to see how deeply her self-worth had been affected by the constant emotional invalidation. At the time, she didn't label it. She simply knew she was drowning and trying to keep a newborn alive while suffocating emotionally.

When she finally left, she was met with silence. Six days went by before her ex even acknowledged she was gone. He didn't ask her to come back. Instead, he vanished—another manipulative tactic known as the "reverse discard." In hindsight, she realizes the distance was a gift. It gave her space to begin healing and to see the relationship for what it truly was.

She had known him since high school. He was the "bad boy" who always found his way back into her life. Looking back, the patterns were always there. Love bombing, gaslighting, boundary-pushing. Each time he reappeared, he never apologized. He just slipped back in, and she let him. She wasn't crazy, but for years she was made to feel like she was. And that kind of emotional manipulation - repeated invalidation, distortion of reality, and lack of empathy is often described by survivors as narcissistic abuse. While Elizabeth never received a formal diagnosis about her former partner, the patterns she uncovered through therapy and research matched much of what others in recovery communities had experienced.

Her real healing began when she sought therapy and started to educate herself. "It was like the floodgates opened," she says. "I found support groups. I found language. I realized I wasn't alone."

Through self-reflection, she connected the dots: she had been attracted to someone who felt familiar - someone with narcissistic tendencies like those she'd seen in parts of her own family. Her father had strong narcissistic traits, and one of her brothers mirrored the same behaviors: controlling, emotionally dismissive, and often passive-aggressive. Spending time with her family during her healing made it impossible to ignore the parallels. Her mother, though loving, had spent her marriage in quiet codependence, constantly adjusting herself to keep the peace. The dynamic had been modeled for her since childhood, and being around it again as an adult made it clear—this wasn't new. It was generational.

Elizabeth saw her younger self in those interactions, and it was a mirror she could no longer look away from.

She started gently pointing out certain patterns to her mom, trying to help her become more aware without overwhelming her. She knew healing couldn't be forced, but she also knew what it felt like to live stuck. And the more Elizabeth understood the root system, the more committed she became to ending it. She could see the same patterns showing up in cousins and other women in the family - marrying men who mirrored what had been modeled to them in childhood.

That's when it hit her: breaking generational patterns wasn't just about who she divorced...it was about who she was becoming. It was about teaching her daughter differently. She started reparenting her child in ways she herself had never experienced - modeling boundaries, validating emotions, encouraging questions, and telling the truth about behavior, even when it came from family.

Elizabeth knew that if her daughter could see narcissistic patterns in a cousin, uncle, or even a grandparent and learn how to respond, she'd be equipped for life. That became part of the healing too, raising a generation who wouldn't have to repeat what she'd been through.

Elizabeth has since become a certified narcissistic abuse recovery coach and works as an elementary school teacher, roles that reflect both her wisdom and her heart for helping others heal. She shows up for her daughter in real-time, modeling healthy boundaries and self-respect, and she shows up for herself by continuing to do the deep work of healing. From journaling and workouts to staying grounded in her faith and seeking support through coaching, Elizabeth built an accountability system that kept her on track through the hardest seasons. She now teaches these same principles to the women she coaches, helping them recognize their patterns, reclaim their power, and take ownership of their growth, one honest step at a time. But she's quick to clarify: "I don't say the abuse was worth it. I say the healing was."

Her faith has been a guiding light through it all. She remembers praying desperately during her pregnancy, not knowing what else to do. And now, with clarity, she sees God's hand in the rescue. One morning, she opened her Bible and read Ephesians 5: "He who loves his wife loves himself." It hit her hard. A narcissist, who truly hates himself, can't possibly love anyone else.

These days, Elizabeth is raising her daughter with tools and truths she never had growing up. She models boundaries, speaks honestly about behavior, and teaches her daughter that she never has to stay in an environment that makes her feel small or unsafe.

For anyone feeling lost in the fog of narcissistic abuse, Elizabeth's story is a reminder: you're not crazy, and you're not alone. You're allowed to step out of the chaos, name what's happening, and walk toward something new.

Her biggest piece of advice? "You can't fix them. But you can absolutely save yourself." Elizabeth is clear: she isn't here to diagnose anyone, but to share her truth. What she experienced was real. Healing became possible the moment she stopped waiting for someone else to change and started choosing herself.

That's what accountability looks like. That's what healing looks like.

Sidebar: Understanding Narcissistic Relationship Patterns

If you've ever felt like you're constantly second-guessing yourself in a relationship. questioning your memory, walking on eggshells, or feeling like you're both the problem and the solution, you're not alone.

Survivors of emotional abuse often find themselves describing similar terms, especially when navigating relationships with individuals who exhibit narcissistic traits. Here are a few common patterns that show up in stories like Elizabeth's:

- **Love Bombing:** Over-the-top displays of affection or attention early in a relationship, often used to create dependency or idealize the partner.
- **Gaslighting:** A form of manipulation where someone denies your reality, making you question your memory, perception, or sanity.
- **Discarding:** Abruptly pushing someone away or ending the relationship once they no longer serve the manipulator's needs.
- **Hoovering:** Attempts to suck a person back into the relationship after a discard, often through flattery, guilt, or false promises of change.
- **Triangulation:** Drawing a third party into the dynamic to create jealousy, insecurity, or competition.

These behaviors don't always point to a clinical diagnosis of narcissistic personality disorder. But they do reflect patterns that many people in emotionally toxic relationships experience. Naming the behaviors without shame, helps survivors validate their reality and begin the work of healing.

Reflection Prompts:

• Where have I been trying to fix or change someone else, instead of focusing on my own healing?

• What patterns from my past am I ready to stop repeating?

• What truth have I been avoiding that's quietly asking me to pay attention?

Action Step: Write down three things you *can* take responsibility for right now. They don't have to be big. Your boundaries. Your reactions. Your healing. Your peace. Accountability won't erase the past, but it will absolutely guide your next step forward.

You are not responsible for someone else's brokenness. But you are responsible for your own healing.

COMPASS FRAMEWORK

SUPPORT

17

ANGELS IN THE WILDERNESS: WHEN SUPPORT FINDS YOU FIRST

"For he will command his angels concerning you to guard you in all your ways." Psalm 91:11 (NIV)

There are seasons where we pour out so much of ourselves that we don't even notice how empty we've become, until we land somewhere completely new, running on fumes. That's where I found myself not long ago: physically, emotionally, and spiritually drained. I had been giving, building, showing up for everyone else, but questioning if I was still on the right path. I didn't trust myself. I was on the verge of giving up.

And then, God met me in the wilderness, again.

This chapter is about **support**. Not just the kind you ask for, but the kind that shows up when you've nearly stopped looking. The kind you don't even realize you need until it's there. Divine detours. Earth angels. Symbols in nature. Confirmation when you're hanging by a thread.

One of my earliest "wilderness moments" happened when I was 20 years old, completely alone in Florida. My car had broken down, and I wandered aimlessly at daybreak, terrified and trying to find someone - *anyone* - who could help. I remember the exact moment I saw a white horse standing in a field. Just beyond it, a home appeared in the distance. That horse led me to safety. A sweet couple answered their door, offered me kindness, and let me use their phone to call for help. I've never forgotten it.

I've had moments like that ever since, where help appeared out of nowhere. Butterflies, rainbows, feathers, initials in the sand. They're not mystical things to me. They're **messages.** I believe God uses creation, people, and perfectly timed circumstances to guide us, refresh us, and remind us that we are not alone.

Scripture says:

"Do not neglect to show hospitality to strangers, for by doing so some have entertained angels without knowing it."
Hebrews 13:2

Sometimes, support shows up in the form of a stranger who helps you and then vanishes. Sometimes it's a phone call at the exact moment you're breaking. Sometimes, it's a sign you didn't ask for, but deeply needed.

When I arrived in Hawaii this year, I was weary. What was meant to be a refreshing retreat came at the tail end of a long stretch of holding space for others. I landed unsure about my next steps, my purpose, and whether any of it was still worth it.

On the very first day, I found a large letter "K" etched in footprints in the sand. That was followed by a butterfly. And then, a rainbow. Back-to-back confirmations. Gentle whispers that God still sees me. That I'm still called. That even when I don't know what's next, He does.

This chapter is about those moments, the **angels in the**

wilderness. The ones who show up when we need a lifeline. The ones who help us breathe again. The signs that we're not crazy for holding on. The whispers from heaven reminding us: **you're not alone, you're not forgotten, and help is already on the way.**

Let that truth carry you into the next story: one of unimaginable grief, mental health struggles, and the sacred, steady support that helped one woman make it through.

Dawn's Story:
Finding Support & Divine Guidance in the Wilderness ▽156

Dawn's journey through the wilderness was one marked by intense struggle, fear, and ultimately, divine protection and unexpected support. Married at 21 to a man who, on the surface, seemed like the ideal partner, she soon found herself trapped in a marriage riddled with mental illness, abuse, and fear. Her husband's severe paranoia, OCD, and erratic behavior created an environment of chaos and control. Despite her hopes for a loving marriage, Dawn quickly realized that her life was spiraling into a nightmare.

Her husband's mental health struggles worsened over time. He became convinced he had AIDS, stemming from an Epstein-Barr virus diagnosis and his past promiscuity. His obsessive behaviors and paranoia dominated their home, leaving Dawn to care for him while trying to maintain a semblance of normalcy. One night she found him standing on the ledge of their terrace, threatening to jump, convinced he couldn't live with his supposed illness. Dawn pleaded with him to come down, calling his sergeant for help. It was one of many moments where her life teetered between safety and tragedy.

Her breaking point came during a terrifying confrontation. One day, while in their bedroom, she noticed him retrieving a magazine clip for an AK-47 hidden under his dresser drawer. When she questioned him, he dismissed her concerns and went to the closet where he had hidden a gun. Realizing the danger, she acted quickly - grabbing her children and rushing them out of the house. "He's going to kill us," she told her mother-in-law as she bundled her kids into the car. In a moment of sheer panic, she tried to flee, but he jumped onto the car, pounding on the windshield as her children sat in the back, terrified.

As she drove away, Dawn spotted a police car stationed on the side of the road. In her panic, instead of stopping, she kept driving. She called her husband's therapist, who urged her to come to his office immediately. While trying to reach safety, her husband pursued her, attempting to run her off the road. Navigating the winding streets, she managed to lose him and continued to the therapist's office. By what she saw as divine intervention, the officer she encountered was the same one who had previously responded to a domestic dispute at her home. "This is God protecting me," she thought, realizing the officer already knew the history of her situation and could take immediate action.

The police were able to apprehend her husband and place him under psychiatric care for 48 hours, which later extended to a week in a facility. During that short window, Dawn took decisive action. She secured an order of protection, found a safe place to live with her children, and informed their schools that her husband was not to be given any information about their whereabouts. She felt as though God had given her a window - a chance to escape the chaos and protect her family.

But the danger wasn't over. When she visited her husband in the facility to inform him about the order of protection, he looked her in the eye and said, "If you think that piece of paper is going to protect you, you're wrong." Despite the chilling threat, she pressed on, supported by her family and a growing sense that divine forces were guiding her steps.

In the months following, Dawn battled anxiety and fear, constantly looking over her shoulder, worried he would find them. She started working from home, doing data entry work to support her children, all while navigating the legal process for custody and protection. The final chapter of her husband's life was a complex mix of tragedy and grace. In the months before his death, a neighbor - a believer - began taking him to church. Dawn noticed a change in him and briefly hoped for reconciliation. But the damage ran deep. On December 9, 2005, after a heavy snowfall that kept the children home from school, she planned for them to visit their father once the roads cleared. But a phone call from a neighbor changed everything. An ambulance arrived at his home, followed by a coroner. Her husband had taken his life.

When she eventually returned to the house, she found his Bible open to Psalm 91, a psalm of protection, and his will placed neatly beside it. In that moment, Dawn realized the depth of his pain and the internal demons he had been battling. Despite everything, she found solace in knowing that he had accepted Christ before his death, believing it was God's way of showing mercy and giving her family a sense of peace.

The aftermath was not easy. She faced blame from her in-laws, the police department, and others who didn't understand the abuse and danger she had endured. But through it all, she clung to her faith. It was her church community, supportive friends, and her deepening relationship with God that carried her through the darkest moments.

Today, Dawn channels her experiences into helping

others. She leads support groups for women who have faced trauma, abuse, and grief, offering them the same kind of guidance and hope that saved her. She speaks openly about her journey, not to dwell on the pain but to highlight the power of resilience, faith, and community.

Her story is a testament to how divine guidance often appears in unexpected ways, through the right person showing up at the right time, through moments of strength when you feel you have none left, and through a sense of purpose that emerges from the deepest pain. Dawn's journey through the wilderness was filled with danger and heartbreak, but it was also marked by moments of undeniable grace.

COMPASS FRAMEWORK

SELF-CARE

18

BEING STILL...
BUT FOR HOW LONG?

"The Lord will fight for you; you need only to be still."
Exodus 14:14 NIV

Let's just go ahead and say it: Being still is freaking hard (at least for this girl).

Especially when you're wired to move, to plan, to *fix*. Especially when your world feels like it's crumbling and you're desperate for answers, any answers. But stillness, real stillness, the kind that connects you with God, the kind that brings peace to the chaos...that's a different kind of strength. That's soul-care.

It took me a long time to realize that self-care isn't always about the outward stuff. It's not always candles and walks and coloring books, though I love those too, and have been known to lead a fun workshop or two using them to demonstrate practical applications of self-care.

Biblical self-care/soul-care is deeper. It's about letting go of control long enough to hear the voice of God. It's trusting that He's working, even when it looks like nothing's moving. It's learning to be still even when every part of you wants to run, fix, or "do." It's learning to take the time to get to know your own inner voice again.

I think about Joseph often when I'm in these seasons. Left in a pit. Forgotten in prison. Thirteen years of wilderness before he ever saw daylight. God didn't just snap His fingers and fix it. Joseph sat in the quiet, the injustice, the ache and oh, the betrayal! And yet it was all part of the preparation. He didn't get to bypass the waiting. And neither do we.

How long will I be here?

That question echoed in my heart more times than I can count. And here's the truth: there's no one-size-fits-all answer. The length of the wilderness isn't about a timeline, it's about transformation. Sometimes it feels like you're going backward, sideways, circling the same old thing over and over again. But healing doesn't move in a straight line.

During my separation, I felt God calling me to be still. Over and over again. I kept trying to move forward, but the doors wouldn't open. I'd ask, *"Do I stay? Do I go?"* I wanted answers, but what I got was silence and songs. I played "Wait on You" by Maverick City Music on loop, crying like it was written just for me.

And not just during that season. Even writing this book required a kind of stillness. I couldn't force it. I had to wait on the words, on the clarity, on the peace to write from a place that felt honest. That's how God works sometimes. He puts us in pause not to punish us, but to prepare us.

I'll be honest, waiting has never been easy for me. I like plans. I like direction. I like knowing what's next. But what I've come to learn is that when I finally stopped striving, I could hear Him more clearly. His Voice wasn't in the noise. It was in the stillness. And when I got quiet enough, I could actually tell the difference between what was mine, what was theirs, and what was God.

What I've learned in the stillness:

- God moves most when I stop trying to.

- My timing is rarely better than His.

- Wisdom grows in the quiet.

- Stillness is not weakness, it's obedience.

Here's something else I've leaned into that's shifted everything:

Meditation - not the trendy version, but the intentional practice of being quiet after you've read the Word, journaled, or prayed. When you pair that stillness with breathwork, something shifts. Focus deepens. Your thoughts begin to slow. You create space to *actually* listen.

Just like you train a muscle, you can train your mind to pause and your body to calm. I've learned to sit with my palms open in silence after reading Scripture, just focusing on my breath and saying, *"Speak, Lord, I'm listening."*

It's not about emptying your mind. It's about filling it with focus.

Mindful concentration + holy stillness = powerful alignment.
This, too, is part of the wilderness. This, too, is part of healing.

Journal + Reflection:

- Have you ever found yourself trying to rush something that just wouldn't move?

- Are there areas in your life right now where God might be inviting you to pause instead of push?

- What might you hear if you gave yourself permission to just *be* for a little while?

Friend, stillness isn't punishment. It's protection. It's a

sacred invitation to slow down, look up, and realign with what matters. You are not forgotten. You are being fortified.

You are not stuck.

You are being still for a reason.

You are taking care of yourself on a deeper level than before.

Let yourself enjoy it, especially if you have loud kids or dogs in your life. If you get a rare moment to be still, soak it in. When you pair stillness with quiet, you are not being lazy. You are practicing peace in action. That kind of peace can shift everything.

A Prayer for Stillness

Lord, I feel lost in this wilderness. The storm feels too heavy to bear, and I don't know what to do. Help me to be still and trust that You are already fighting for me. Give me the courage to stand firm and the faith to believe in Your plan, even when I can't see it. Amen.

19

GROUNDED GRATITUDE

"Gratitude doesn't change the storm—it changes the one walking through it."
—Unknown

Gratitude has this way of completely transforming your perspective. In my opinion, it's a radical form of self-care. It's like finding a clear trail in the middle of a wilderness you thought you'd never escape. When you take the time to reflect on what you're grateful for, even in the messiest seasons of life, you reclaim your power. You're saying, *"Yes, this hard thing happened, but I'm still standing, and there's still good here."*

Let me share something personal. My ex-husband now lives just around the corner from me. I could have allowed that reality to ruin me. I could have fixated on the pain of our failed marriage and the hurt I carried from those years. But I made a different choice. I decided to shift my focus, not because the hurt didn't happen, but because he is no longer the source of my pain. God is the source of my peace.

Instead of seeing his presence as a trigger for my past, I see it as an opportunity to be grateful. I'm grateful my girls are happier now that their dad is close by. They're not crying themselves to sleep because they miss him. Their joy means more to me than my own discomfort. And honestly, that's the power of gratitude - not denying the hard stuff but choosing to see the good that comes alongside it.

Gratitude has also taught me to appreciate the boundaries I've built since he moved closer. I can be thankful for the peace I've created in my life, even as I navigate this new dynamic. Gratitude isn't always about celebrating the obvious wins. Sometimes, it's about recognizing the quiet victories - like reclaiming your peace and finding joy despite the chaos.

For the longest time, I thought gratitude and self-care was about the easy stuff - the sunshine, the good days, the bubble baths, getting a pedicure, the little joys. And those things matter, but real gratitude goes deeper. It's being thankful for the hard things, the heartbreaks, and the moments that nearly broke you, because they're the very things that shape you.

I remember waking up on my 50th birthday, newly divorced, and feeling like everything was over. The pain of starting over at that age felt unbearable. But as the days passed, I started to see things differently. Instead of saying, '*My life is over at 50*', I began to say, '*I get to start over at 50*'. And what a gift that turned out to be. To start fresh with wisdom, experience, and a heart that had been through the fire - it became something to celebrate. It's my biggest gratitude "flex"!

It's like the way I changed the way I look at my health journey and the way it's changed my perspective on everything:

I used to have a goal *weight*. Now I have a **_GOAL LIFE_**.

That's what gratitude does. It helps you take those seeds of sorrow and turn them into roots of joy. It doesn't erase the pain, but it reminds you that the pain has purpose. The person you're becoming wouldn't exist without the struggles you've endured. And even though it's hard to see it in the moment, those challenges are leveling you up for something greater. The definition of joy is not related to a constant state of happiness, that would be unrealistic. The biblical application of the word joy is actually translated to be aligned with the word Strength.

Joy is a gift that flows from being in God's presence. As Psalm 16:11 reminds us, it's in His presence that we find the fullness of joy. This isn't the fleeting kind of happiness that depends on circumstances - it's something deeper, something lasting.

Nehemiah 8:10 tells us that the joy of the Lord is our strength. It's the power that keeps us standing when life tries to knock us down. It's how people can say things like - "I don't know how I made it through it, it's like something was holding me up the entire time." Joy doesn't mean the lack of suffering; in fact, it often emerges most profoundly after seasons of grief and trial. Psalm 30:5 reminds us that while weeping may endure for a night, joy comes in the morning.

Even in hardships, joy can be present. James 1:2 says to consider it pure joy when we face challenges because those moments shape us, teaching us perseverance and faith. This kind of joy feels so countercultural, doesn't it? In a world that tells us to chase happiness, joy rooted in trials and faith can feel almost impossible.

But here's the truth: God never promised happiness as the world defines it. He knows that the fall of man introduced brokenness into the world, making perfect happiness impossible. What He does promise is something far greater. He promises that He has overcome the world, and through Him, joy is always accessible.

Does God want us to be unhappy? Of course not. But He understands that life will bring seasons of pain, uncertainty, and sadness. The question isn't whether we'll face those seasons, it's where we'll turn when we do. Will we chase the temporary heights of happiness, or will we anchor ourselves in the enduring joy that comes from Him? Joy is what sustains us. It's what gives us the strength to rise each day, knowing that our hope is not tied to what's fleeting but to what is eternal.

This kind of joy is an invitation. It is a call to live differently, to see beyond the surface, and to root ourselves in a deeper truth. It's not easy, but it is worth everything. And it's available to you, no matter where you are or what you're facing.

Gratitude doesn't always come easily. It requires stillness, a willingness to pause, reflect, and allow the process to unfold. During the first year after my divorce, I clung to the song *Gratitude* by Brandon Lake. It became my anthem, a reminder to stay patient and trust God's timing, even when nothing around me made sense. Some days I didn't even have the words to pray. That song spoke for me.

One part that always gave me chills was the line about throwing up your hands and roaring like a lion. That imagery stopped me every time. I've always loved lions. There's something about their power and presence that makes you pay attention. They don't need to prove anything. They simply stand in who they are. In that season, I didn't feel powerful at all. I felt tired, small, and emotionally raw. But that line reminded me that even when I had nothing fancy to offer, my praise still mattered. It could be messy. It could be whispered. Or it could roar through my tears.

Gratitude in the wilderness is not about pretending everything is okay. It is about saying thank you even when your voice shakes. It is the kind of gratitude that sounds like a roar. It may not be polished or perfect, but it is honest and full of faith. That roar became my praise, and it was enough.

What I didn't fully understand at the time was that praise isn't just a nice gesture. It's a weapon. In the middle of heartbreak, confusion, and fear, praise shifts the atmosphere. It reminds the enemy that even when we're weary, we're still worshiping. Psalm 22:3 tells us that God inhabits the praises of His people. He doesn't wait for us to get it all together first. He shows up right in the middle of our mess, our tears, and our surrender.

Stillness isn't passive; it's active trust. It's saying, *I don't have all the answers, but I know the One who does.* And honestly, not knowing the full picture is intentional. If we saw everything that was coming, we'd probably feel too overwhelmed to handle it. Being still allows us to focus on what's right in front of us and let God work on the bigger plan.

For me, this stillness showed up in journaling and reflection. Writing helped me untangle the chaos in my mind and make space for gratitude. It reminded me that even in the mess, there's something to be thankful for. Gratitude starts in those moments of stillness, when you choose to see the good amidst the hard.

Your story, with all its twists and turns, is part of your legacy. Gratitude isn't about pretending the pain didn't happen. It's about recognizing that God has used those experiences to grow you into who you are today. I want you to know that the hard things you've gone through...those heartbreaks, those moments that felt impossible - they don't define you. They refine you. And when you lean into gratitude, you'll start to see that the struggle was never wasted. Here's how you can begin to find gratitude in your story:

1. **Reflect on the Hard Things**: Write down one challenge you've faced recently. Ask yourself, *What have I learned from this? How has it shaped me?*

2. **Celebrate Small Wins**: Gratitude doesn't have to be grand. Start with something simple, like acknowledging that you got through a tough day.

3. **Shift Your Perspective:** Think about a decision you made that protected your peace or honored your growth. Even if no one else saw it, it mattered. Let that reminder fuel your gratitude.

Gratitude is a powerful anchor in the wilderness. It doesn't take away the pain, but it gives you something steady to hold onto. Gratitude says, *"This hard thing happened, but it's not the whole story. God is still working in my life."*

If you're in a hard season, I want to encourage you to lean into gratitude. It's not about ignoring the bad - it's about choosing to see the good. It's about trusting that the wilderness is shaping you for something better, something brighter. Gratitude gives you the strength to keep going, even when the path feels uncertain.

A Prayer for Gratitude and Peace

Lord, I thank You for the lessons You're teaching me, even in the hard times. Help me to be still, to listen, and to trust Your plan. Show me the good that still exists, even when life feels overwhelming. Give me the courage to embrace gratitude and let it guide me toward healing, hope, and joy. Amen.

PART 3:
REACHING THE
PROMISED LAND

20
FINDING YOURSELF AGAIN

"For the Spirit God gave us does not make us timid, but gives us power, love and self-discipline".
2 Timothy 1:7

Starting over at 50 felt like standing in front of a mirror I didn't recognize. I had spent so many years being someone's wife, someone's mother, someone's employee... that I wasn't quite sure who *I* was without those titles.

I remember thinking, "It's too late to reinvent myself." That fear was real. But deep down, I started to question it. What if that was just a story I had been telling myself? What if my identity wasn't behind me... but still waiting to be discovered?

This chapter of my life wasn't about survival anymore. It was about becoming.

Becoming someone I hadn't met yet but was finally ready to be.

Here's the thing. I finally recognized that I was not starting from scratch.

I was starting from **experience**. I had to use what I'd learned to move forward.

I built routines I committed to and made dedicated to showing up for myself every day first. When I would find myself slipping back into my old habits or routines, I would gently ask myself the question, "Does this line up with the life I'm committed to live?" because if it didn't, I decided a FIRM NO to anything that wasn't that. But I really had to get to know myself. My reflection felt like a stranger at first. Your identity changes after major life shifts. The people you used to spend the most time with shift and so do your routines and patterns. For me, it wasn't just the loss of my marriage; it was the loss of my identity. I had defined myself by my roles: wife, mother, entrepreneur, and all the dynamics changed for me once the ink on the divorce papers dried, causing me to spiral wildly off course.

If I didn't change, I might have ended up dead. That's not an exaggeration. That was the reality knocking on the door of my exhaustion and despair. I didn't want my kids to carry the memory of a mom who gave up. But I was terrified to take the first step. I remember thinking, *I don't have time to focus on myself. I have kids to raise, bills to pay, and a life that's unraveling by the hour.*

Self-care felt like a luxury I couldn't afford, and healing felt completely out of reach. But the truth hit me one day with full force. I couldn't become the mother, the leader, or the woman I knew I was meant to be if I kept putting myself last. I was burning out, emotionally and physically. That's when I had to accept that survival mode was no longer serving me. I had to stop pretending I could pour from an empty cup. I had to give myself permission to matter. A lot of this stemmed from feeling unworthy of that, and I had to do some serious reconditioning of my mind and heart to believe that I had great worth in God's eyes and my own.

So, I did something that felt bold and uncomfortable. I started dating myself. I took myself to dinner, went to the movies alone, and wandered around the stores without a mission or a timer. I would walk or jog the beach day in and day out, every chance I could. I wasn't doing it to prove anything. I was trying to remember who I was outside of trying to be the perfect wife or the over-functioning mom. At first, it felt awkward and unfamiliar. I caught myself reaching for my phone to avoid being present. But eventually, I started to enjoy my own company again. I laughed out loud. I goofed around. I allowed myself to be silly again. I remembered what I liked. I found pieces of myself I didn't even know I had lost.

Out of that rediscovery came purpose. I built a business that gave meaning to the pain I had walked through. *The Wilderness Compass* became my way of turning heartbreak into hope. I wasn't just telling my story. I was living proof that it's possible to rebuild. I found healing, and now I get to help others navigate their own wilderness with tools I had to learn the hard way.

I didn't just carry pain in my heart. I carried it in my body, too. Releasing that weight, both physically and emotionally, was one of the most freeing parts of my journey. I created habits that aligned with the life I wanted, not just the one I was trying to survive. I let go of things that dulled my clarity and replaced them with choices that gave me strength. The more I honored myself with consistency, the more my life began to transform.

Today, I'm healthier, stronger, and more fulfilled than I've ever been. But getting here took work. I had to choose myself when it felt selfish. I had to walk away from old patterns that once felt safe. I had to say yes to a version of me I hadn't even met yet. It took honesty, grace, and courage to keep stepping forward. But I made it. And now,

I help others believe they can, too.

But let me be clear. Life didn't suddenly become perfect. I didn't walk into some sunshine-filled version of reality where everything was easy and nothing ever went wrong. Healing doesn't mean you never struggle again. It means you now have tools, self-awareness, and faith to face the hard days without falling apart. I still have moments of fear, frustration, and fatigue. I still battle doubt and have to reset my mindset more often than I'd like to admit. But now, I catch myself quicker. I speak kinder to myself. I don't spiral the way I used to. That is the real win.

This version of my life is not perfect, but it is peaceful. And that peace didn't come from everything working out. It came from deciding I was worth the work it takes to keep showing up for myself - even when it's messy, even when it's hard, and especially when it's quiet.

You are not too far gone. You are not behind. You don't need to have it all figured out. You just need to believe that you are worth the fight. One small step forward can change everything.

Journal & Reflect:

• What version of you have you been trying to find again?

• What small action today can support the life you're committed to creating?

• Where have you been showing up out of obligation instead of alignment?

21

REFLECTION IN THE MIRROR - A JOURNEY TO RECLAIMING SELF

BY CASSIE LENNOX

I'll never forget that moment, looking in the mirror, unable to recognize the tearstained face staring back at me. The sparkle in her eyes was dim, the smile looked forced, and everything about her was missing something. Authenticity, perhaps.

"Who have you become?" I asked myself, waiting for a reply that only came back with questions and confusion. The more I wondered how I got lost, the more lost I felt.

Stuck in a loveless marriage, having been best friends before that, I convinced myself that this would work and things would fall into place somehow, but that was not the case. We were very different people on very different pages, with conflicting beliefs on what a relationship and marriage should be. I spent years hanging onto the last strands of hope that things would somehow suddenly shift. But I have learned that compromise is not the same as expecting others to change. Not by far.

I was disengaged from my friends and my family, and even my relationship with myself was gradually fading. So gradual, that I barely noticed it, or perhaps didn't have the time to acknowledge it, or maybe just didn't want to. The friendships that remained were only through social media. I was developing social anxiety from feeling sheltered for so long. I had nothing but my children and my words. Writing was my only escape, the pen my last friend.

I was questioning my purpose and if I really had it in me to achieve those hopes and dreams, to make myself into everything my 8-year-old self had declared she'd be, to impact the world, if I couldn't even take my own advice. I could write beautiful words that inspired others. Yet, where was that inspiration taking ME?

I was a broken woman who was motivating others. The imposter syndrome was real.

The downward spiral had been a process for numerous years, losing touch with my authenticity. Not having boundaries, allowing others and false labels to dictate my life, what I could do, who I could be. I was letting life happen "to me." Unknowingly, playing victim in my own story.

The more time passed, the further away from myself I got. Losing friends since I never spent time with them, no longer doing the things I loved to do, no longer believing in myself as I once had. The confidence had faded, the fire had smoldered, and I felt like a prisoner, too weak to bend the bars, too scared to even try.

Was this rock bottom? I swore I had writing that suggests I've been here before, over and over. No one knows how many times.

But this time... this time I fixated on my reflection. I stared at that image of who I'd become for I don't know how long. Long enough to stare into my own eyes, forcing myself to remember what is, and imagining what could be beyond that moment. What could be if I made a change.

And I vowed to make that change.

It was the one vow in my life that made all the difference.

It was time to move forward, onward. That decision, and the refusal to back down, no matter what it took. To have discernment, allow time, always in forward motion, always showing grace to myself.

And so, I began to create my plan.

I outlined the steps. I wrote it all down. I made a non-negotiable to-do list.

The whole time knowing, that reflection in the mirror was counting on me, and her sad eyes had cried enough tears. She was ready to have that sparkle again.

I know I had to leap out of my comfort zone. I had to shift my mindset and treat each challenge as an opportunity, celebrate each milestone, and be open to the possibilities.

Did it all go exactly as planned? No.

I have overused the roller coaster analogy my whole life... but this time I embraced it, because I understood that stepping away, leaving, moving on, whatever you want to call it, was going to be a crazy ride.

It wasn't about the thrill at the moment... but I was so looking towards the moment I saw something beyond this.

When I took that key...

And unlocked the front door, seeing my new apartment for the first time... MY apartment.

It was empty. It was bare. It was a blank page. A new chapter.

And it was all MINE.

My heart filled with a sense of excitement and forward motion that was beyond anything I've known in so long.

I felt freedom, for the first time.

I felt pride.

I felt self-love.

I felt hope. Determination. Possibilities.

Now when I look in the mirror, in my own bathroom, in my own apartment, in MY own life, I see a resemblance to the girl I used to be.

But she's grown up now. In mind, spirit, and heart.

She's still healing, but the sparkle is back in her eyes. The smile is present. She doesn't have a perfect path, but she isn't lost. She is navigating her truth. Collecting her authenticity with each passing moment, with each step forward.

While I'm in a different season of wilderness now, I'm not that woman anymore. I hold my head higher, I shift my thinking, I show myself more grace, and navigate with a stronger sense of understanding the beauty that comes with each milestone of forward motion.

And everytime I turn the key and step into my apartment, with all my furniture and belongings and things that represent myself, and every moment of my kids' laughter within these walls, I thank God for the strength, perseverance, and trust in myself to push on and do what I knew was right.

Sometimes I still feel a bit of panic remembering how scary it was to take the necessary steps. But I also feel the self-pride and dignity that comes with the decision to pick yourself up and make yourself proud.

Now, my heart is open. Someday I will find love, knowing what I want, what I need, and what I deserve in a relationship.
My friends are plenty, and the best I could ask for. They lift me up, we spend time and laughter, share growth, and can be genuine with each other. I am also my own friend again.

That impact? You better believe I'm going to make it. 8-year-old me will be proud. She already is.

It all comes back to that one decision. Decide that it's time to regain yourself. Commit to yourself. When we are at our best, we do better not just for our own story, but better for our family, friends, and for the world.

Take some time each day to look in the mirror at your reflection. Notice the sparkle, the smile, and all that is whole. Pep-talk her if you need to. Remind her that she is loved. And always be ready to support her and take her hand as you navigate the wilderness.

22

DECIDING THE LIFE YOU WANT TO LIVE & LIVING IT

"The only person you are destined to become is the person you decide to be" Ralph Waldo Emerson

Facing my fears, I asked myself simple yet life-altering questions: "If I could build the life I truly wanted, what would it look like? Who would I become?" The decision marked a turning point for me, sparking a commitment to heal from the inside out. As you reflect on your own journey, I invite you to ask yourself similar questions. What challenges are you currently facing, and how can you use them as opportunities to create the life you've always wanted?

One of the biggest hurdles many of us face, especially after a chapter ends (including divorce), is failing to pause. We often jump from one chapter of life to the next without giving ourselves time to process. That lack of space to heal can be dangerous. When we don't allow ourselves the time to realign our inner compass, we risk making decisions based on distraction or convenience rather than intentionality.

I've been there. I've rushed into situations to avoid feeling lonely, hurt, or grieving. Instead of doing the hard work of healing, I sought temporary fixes that only prolonged my pain. Looking back, I can see how those choices led me into years of unnecessary struggle.

Without time to process and grow, we often repeat old patterns or make choices that don't serve us well.

I once told my daughter it takes a full year to truly know someone. You need time to see them in all seasons of life, to observe how they handle both joy and adversity. Rushing into relationships or major decisions without this time can lead to situations that aren't healthy or aligned with the person you're striving to become. While some people find success in quick decisions, my experience has shown me that taking the time to heal and reflect creates a stronger foundation for the future.

Honoring yourself means intentionally deciding what you need to heal and move forward. Many women, myself included, have struggled with facing the hard truths about what went wrong in past relationships or why we accepted less than we deserved. Instead of sitting with those feelings, it can be tempting to move on quickly, distracting ourselves from the pain. However, true growth only happens when we stop, reflect, and do the inner work.

For me, this realization came after years of ignoring the signs. I numbed myself in various ways and avoided dealing with the root causes of my struggles. When I finally decided to honor myself, I started creating space to ask the tough questions about what I wanted my life to look like. This shift was uncomfortable at first, but it was the most freeing decision I ever made.

Deciding the life you want to live means being intentional about every aspect of it. This includes the people you surround yourself with, how you spend your time, and the energy you allow into your space. It also involves visualizing what your days look like and planning for the future you want to create. When I began to focus on these details, my life changed dramatically. I took a different approach by reverse engineering the life I desired and working to build it once I knew what I wanted.

I started each day with movement, meditation, and positive affirmations. I became more mindful about what I fed my mind and body, and I tracked my progress through journaling and habit trackers. These practices allowed me to stay focused on my goals and reminded me that every step, no matter how small, mattered. Progress isn't always linear, and I still have days when I stumble, but I've learned to appreciate the lessons in those moments.

I also had a wonderful coach ask me some great questions that I often ask my own clients now since they helped me so much. What's the one thing, that if by achieving that, everything else becomes a little easier? And what is one thing we can do to start that process today? For me, in the beginning, it was getting healthier, and it started with one step. Walking, one day at a time. I knew getting healthy would help me find my confidence in a new way to help me move into doing other things that I've always wanted to do. Guess what? I'm doing them right now. You can, too!

We often get so caught up in the end result that we forget about the small, consistent steps required to get there. Whether it's creating a healthier lifestyle, building financial stability, or cultivating meaningful relationships, success is built on daily habits. For me, this meant shifting my mindset, surrounding myself with supportive people, and being patient with myself when I faltered.

There was a time when I believed quick fixes could solve my problems. I tried every fast action diet for decades and even underwent weight loss surgery back in

2015, thinking it would change everything overnight. But the reality is that sustainable change requires more than a single action. My weight would yoyo within weeks or months of inconsistency. Real change demands commitment, self-awareness, and a willingness to stay the course even when progress feels non-existent or slow. We are making internal changes that require foundational correction. This takes time and consistent actions that become habits.

When I finally approached my health and life with intentionality, everything began to fall into place. In January of 2023 I began a long-term fix lifestyle-minded weight loss journey and now I've lost 60lbs and have kept it off for over 2 years now. What a difference when you make your habits align with your why and ensure you understand the steps you're taking along while having a clear expectation of the outcome.

To create the life you want, you need to envision your promised land. What does it look like? How does it feel? Who is there with you? Start by writing it down. Be bold and specific about your dreams. Picture your ideal day, the people who uplift you, and the goals you want to achieve. Then, break those dreams into actionable steps. Most importantly, what does it look like when things get in the way of staying consistent? What does your commitment look like when you don't feel like doing it? Can you envision yourself doing it even when it's hard? You don't see that part on many vision boards. What does walking in the cold rain feel like vs. walking in the warm sunshine? With each small accomplishment, you'll move closer to the life you've envisioned.

You have the power to design your life. By taking the time to heal, setting intentions, and committing to the process, you can create a future filled with purpose and joy. It's not always easy, but it's worth every effort.

The Lord tells us to be strong and courageous in Joshua 1:9. We just need to take the first step because He promises to be with us wherever we go.

Suzanne's Story: A Daughter's Promise

"Do not remember the former things, Nor consider the things of old.
Behold, I will do a new thing, Now it shall spring forth;
Shall you not know it?
I will even make a road in the wilderness And rivers in the desert."
Isaiah 43:18-19.

It started during COVID. Suzanne's mom was still walking, still functioning on the outside, but her anxiety was through the roof and no one could quite figure out why. As a nurse, Suzanne had always stepped up to help when her aging mother and stepfather needed support. But this felt different. Heavier. Off.

When Suzanne and her husband bought a new house, they renovated the entire downstairs with the plan for her parents to move in. But when they showed them the home, her stepfather exploded.

"I'm not moving in there," he snapped, bitter and angry.

Suzanne looked over at her mother, who was sitting quietly, but with terror in her eyes.

"Mom, do you want to come live with us?" Suzanne asked.

And with a quiet, shaky voice, her mother answered:

"I'm done. I want out. I want to be with you and Dave."

What was supposed to be a blended family living arrangement turned into a full-on intervention. Suzanne and her husband went back to her mom's house under the guise of a short visit — just a few days to "see how she adjusts." But they knew. They slipped out clothes, medications, and essentials without stirring suspicion.

Her mom settled into a simple back bedroom in their home, a recliner, a small TV, a dresser and looked around, finally able to exhale.

"I didn't know what it was like to not be screamed at every day," she told Suzanne.

That was the moment Suzanne knew this wasn't just about caregiving. This was about rescuing her mom.

From that day forward, Suzanne became her mother's legal, emotional, and physical advocate. A friend at the gym connected her to an elder law attorney, and with her mother's early dementia setting in, Suzanne made sure to ask for her consent again and again.

Every time, her mom was clear: "I don't want to be married to him anymore. I'm done."

But Suzanne knew the next step would be the hardest.

"You have to tell him," she said. "It has to come from you."

They sat across from him together. Suzanne's mom was shaking like a child. But she found the courage, looked him in the eye, and said, "I want a divorce."

That's when the war began.

He raged. He blamed Suzanne for everything. He hurled cruel words and manipulative threats. Suzanne's husband, Dave, tried to be the neutral middleman, even retrieving mail and necessities until one day he'd had enough. After a blowup involving a family heirloom, he was done. The emotional weight of the situation had reached a breaking point for all of them.

Meanwhile, Suzanne's mother continued to decline. Her body weakened. Her mind drifted. The dementia advanced, and the legal battle dragged on. But Suzanne was relentless. She secured a new attorney, a woman who fiercely protected her mother's interests and pushed forward.

In October, the divorce was finalized. Suzanne's mom passed away in December.

But those final weeks were sacred. Hospice was brought in. A caregiver named Debbie, another Godsend, came into their lives and gave Suzanne the ability to work again, while knowing her mom was safe and cared for.

That last Sunday, Suzanne finally made it to church. She had been afraid to leave her mother alone on weekends, but her friend urged her to go. That morning, the pastor began speaking about heaven unplanned, unexpected, and so very needed. He painted a picture of streets of gold and peace beyond understanding.

When Suzanne returned home, her mother asked, "Where were you?"

"I went to church," she said. "And the pastor talked about heaven."

Her mother's eyes softened. "That sounds nice," she said.

That night, her breathing changed. Her pulse dropped. Suzanne asked if she wanted her to sleep in the room with her. Her mom said no.

The next morning, she was gone.

She had died in peace, no yelling, no fear, just freedom. And the timing? Her final wish for the divorce had been granted just weeks before. Suzanne said her mom rallied for about a month after that. It was as if the weight had lifted, and she knew she had finally won.

Suzanne kept her promise. She never put her mother in a nursing home. She cleaned her, fed her, and fought for her until the very end.

There were moments when she nearly gave up. When she wondered if the fight was even worth it. But one day, her mother looked her straight in the eye and said:

"Please don't give up. You kids deserve to have something I worked so hard for. If you give up, he gets everything. And he wins."

So, Suzanne put the gloves back on. And she fought. Not just for what was fair but for what was right.

Today, Suzanne says this chapter of her life wasn't about grief. It was about **love that never gave up.** Her mom taught her how to fight, how to forgive, and how to finish well.

And she passed that fire on to her daughter.

23

THE PROMISED LAND

"I will restore to you the years that the swarming locust has eaten." Joel 2:25

The wilderness journey is not without purpose. It leads us to the Promised Land – a place of fulfillment, peace, and joy. The Promised Land is different for everyone; it may be a state of mind, a physical place, or a sense of accomplishment and contentment. The key is to believe that this land exists and that you are being guided towards it. Embrace the journey, trust the process, and have faith that you will reach your Promised Land.

The spaces we inhabit and the influences we allow into our lives have a profound impact on our healing and growth. Over the last few weeks, I made a conscious decision to adjust the energy around me, starting with something as seemingly small as my workout playlists. I realized certain types of music were pulling me into a negative headspace. The lyrics, the tone, and the memories they evoked were not serving me. Once I swapped those songs for uplifting and energizing music, I noticed an immediate shift. My workouts became a time of motivation and clarity instead of a trigger for frustration or sadness.

It's the same with any element of our environment. Negative energy, whether it comes from a playlist, a cluttered room, or toxic interactions, can seep into our minds and bodies. Healing starts with the spaces we create and the intentional choices we make about what surrounds us. Think about the places you spend the most time. Do they inspire you, recharge you, or provide peace? Or are they filled with chaos and reminders of pain?

To move toward your promised land, you need to envision what it looks like and map it out in your mind. What kind of space makes you feel inspired and whole? What changes can you make to your environment to foster healing, health, and peace? Maybe it's as simple as clearing clutter, adding a plant to brighten your space, or replacing negative influences with uplifting ones. Surround yourself with elements that remind you of where you want to go, not where you've been.

Your environment can either fuel your journey or hold you back. The choice is yours to create a space that reflects the life you are building, one that aligns with your vision for healing and growth.

The most recent phase of my journey wasn't just about surviving; it was about thriving. I realized that my life didn't end at 50. At 50, starting over felt daunting. I thought, "It's too late for me to change my life. I'm too old to reinvent myself now." But I realized that this was just a story I was telling myself. Age is just a number, and I had the power to create a new life at any age. If I didn't take action then, I would only regret it later. It was just beginning. I committed to creating a life that reflected who I was now, not the person I was before. I built a new business! One that allows me to serve women who are going through the same struggles I had faced.

The Wilderness Compass became my way of turning my pain into purpose. I could use my story, my experience, and my newfound strength to guide others. I also prioritized my physical health. I lost over sixty pounds and transformed my body through consistent movement and healthy eating. I haven't had a drop of alcohol since December 2022. But even more than that, I transformed my mind. I started building routines and habits that aligned with the life I wanted to live.

I began asking myself daily, *"Does this action support the life I'm committed to creating?"* If the answer was no, I learned to say no without guilt because my new identity didn't align with the actions the old me used to take. I had to learn to say out loud, *"That's not who I am anymore. I'm this..."* (insert the new identity that matches the healthier version you are becoming or have become).

For instance, I'm not on a diet. I'm an active, healthy person who eats well most of the time and enjoys indulgence on special occasions.

Today, I am healthier, stronger, and more fulfilled than ever. But the journey was not easy. It required relentless effort, self-love, and the willingness to step into the unknown.

Now, I'm using my story to help other women navigate their own transformations. You don't have to do it alone. If I can rebuild my life, so can you.

We can glow forward together.

24

JESUS - OUR TRUE NORTH

For those who share my faith, Jesus is the ultimate guide through the wilderness. He is our True North. He is the steady, unchanging point of reference that keeps us grounded when everything around us feels uncertain. Turning to Jesus in times of struggle is not just about obedience. It is about trust. It is about believing that even when nothing makes sense, He still does.

I have seen it in my own life and in the lives of so many others. When I was in my wilderness season, I did not need more opinions, more noise, or more distractions. I needed direction. I needed peace. And that is exactly what I found when I started turning to Him more intentionally. His love, His teachings, and His Word gave me something solid to hold onto. The terrain around me did not change overnight, but I stopped spinning in circles.

When Jesus was led into the wilderness (Matthew 4:1–11), He faced real pain, real temptation, and real isolation. And He did not run from it. He met it head-on. He showed us how to stay grounded in truth, how to stay connected to the Father, and how to speak life when the enemy tried to tear Him down. That was not just an example. It was an invitation.

In response, I began to model it. I prayed even when I was tired. I opened my Bible even when it felt dry. I created space for silence and stillness even when it was uncomfortable. And even though I was not always consistent, I kept returning. I kept returning to Him.

There were days when temptation showed up too. The temptation to numb out. To give up. To go back to habits or relationships that felt familiar but were never really healthy. In those moments, I had to pause and speak the truth over myself. I would say aloud, "I do not do that anymore. I am a spiritually connected daughter of the Most High King who spends time with her Father."

I reminded myself that I was not walking alone. I was being led by Someone who knew exactly where I was going. The more time I spent with Him, the more I craved the things that came from Him. Peace. Wisdom. Clarity. Healing.

Around mid-2023, I started hearing a phrase that was gaining momentum in self-help and personal growth circles: "Let them." Mel Robbins popularized it, and it has resonated with so many people, including me. The idea is simple and powerful. Let them go. Let them pull away. Let them misunderstand. Let them live how they choose. Let them be who they are without chasing, explaining, or fixing.

And there is some truth in that. Sometimes freedom comes not from holding on tighter, but from releasing the need to be understood or approved of. Letting go can protect our peace.

But as a woman of faith, I realized something even more important. Before we let them, we must first Let Him.

Let Him tell us who we are.

Let Him lead us into healing.

Let Him shape our boundaries and soften our hearts.

Let Him show us how to let go without bitterness.

Let Him strengthen us for what is next.

Letting them walk away may create space but letting Him in creates transformation.

Let them is wise. Let Him is holy. One sets you free from people. The other sets you free within yourself. When I finally stopped asking, "What do they think?" and started asking, "What does He say?" everything shifted.

When we say, "*As for me and my house, we will serve the Lord*" (Joshua 24:15), we are not just making a bold statement of belief. We are choosing our direction. We are saying, "Even here. Even now. I will follow."

And when we follow Jesus, we are not only walking toward healing. We are walking toward purpose.

So, if you find yourself in the wilderness right now, take heart. You do not have to fix everything today. You do not need all the answers. Just take one step. One breath. One prayer. One moment of stillness. Let go of what was never meant to define you. And let Him meet you right where you are.

He always does.

CONCLUSION
THE WAY FORWARD

What is the wilderness? What does it mean to you? Is it heartbreak? Grief? A transition you did not choose? A season of waiting, or the long, lonely road of rebuilding from the ground up?

The wilderness can feel like being stuck, scared, or silently unraveling in a world that keeps spinning. It can feel like being unworthy, unsure, unmoored. But here's what I've learned, and what every page of *Wilderness Wisdom* has whispered to you along the way:

You are not alone.

Wilderness Wisdom isn't just a book of stories. It's a lifeline, woven from the real experiences of women who've stood right where you're standing: tired, trembling, or totally lost...and still found their way through. These are women who've faced divorce, loss, illness, soul-deep uncertainty, and the ache of starting over. And in the middle of all that, they found clarity. Courage. Faith. A new way forward.

Each chapter was designed to walk you through one of the core elements of the **COMPASS Framework**: **Community, Openness, Mindset, Purposeful Movement, Accountability, Support, and Self-Care**. These aren't just concepts. They are trail markers. Tools. Anchors. Sacred reminders that even when life feels wild and uncharted, you can still find your footing.

These strategies helped me rebuild my life piece by piece. They helped me take ownership of my healing. They reminded me of who I was, before the storm, and who I was becoming.

I created systems to track progress when my days blurred together. I leaned on family and a safe community when I felt like giving up. I wrote goals that scared me, and I let others lovingly hold me to them. I stopped waiting for someone else to change and started choosing me. Again. And again.

This book is your compass. Not because it tells you exactly where to go, but because it helps you pause and ask, "Where am I now, and where do I want to be?"

The wilderness can feel like the end of the road. But it's often the beginning of something sacred.

You don't need a perfect plan - just the next right step. And if you let faith guide your journey, if you let resilience rise even in the quiet moments, you'll find your way through. Not around. Not over. But through.

And when you do, when you take that final step out of the fog and into the light- you won't just be found. You'll be transformed. Isaiah 61:3 says that God wants to give us beauty for ashes - but if we want beauty, what's the one thing we need to do with our ashes?

Give them to God. For when we do, we are planting them to grow into trees of righteousness, for the purpose of his Glory. That's it friend - that's the goal, to show the world the transformation we can achieve through the miraculous transformation of taking the seeds of our sorrow and turning them into glorious, beautiful new creations wrapped in the light garment of joy, of praise, in exchange for the heaviness those ashes represented.

Ohhhh to feel light again! I tell you - it is where the most majestic power resides. How do I know? When people look at me now and talk with me they notice my joy and the lightness of my soul. I used to be HEAVY in more than one sense of the word. I have embraced the journey that led to my brokenness and have released the fear of allowing it to define my future. That is True Freedom and it is available to you as well.

"To console those who mourn in Zion, To give them beauty for ashes, The oil of joy for mourning, The garment of praise for the spirit of heaviness; That they may be called trees of righteousness, The planting of the LORD, that He may be glorified." Isaiah 61:3

This is your invitation. To believe again. To begin again. To keep walking. I'm right here, totally cheering you on along with the rest of the women who contributed to this adventure. There is power in Community. Don't forget that. We are yours. As they say here in the South, "Welcome in!"

Your wilderness doesn't define you. But what you do next just might.

What's one way you can take action and physically represent what you're doing with your ashes?

You can buy a piece of seed paper, write your "ashes" and then bury and plant them... and grow something beautiful.

Scripture to Anchor You:

"The Lord will guide you always; He will satisfy your needs in a sun-scorched land and will strengthen your frame. You will be like a well-watered garden, like a spring whose waters never fail."

Isaiah 58:11

Reflection Questions:

- Where am I now on my journey through the wilderness?

- What has this season taught me about myself, my strength, or my faith?

- Which part of the **COMPASS Framework** do I feel most drawn to right now?

- Who can I invite into my tribe to walk with me from here?

Blessing: May you walk out of this wilderness more rooted than ever before. May clarity rise where confusion once lived. May you find peace that surpasses all understanding. And may you remember, always, you are never alone. Keep going. Your promised land is ahead. Psalm 46:5 says, '*God is within her, she will not fall.*' And the women and I in this book are standing here today as proof of that.

Next Steps on Your Journey

Your wilderness season is not the end of your story. It is the start of something sacred.

My hope is that *Wilderness Wisdom* has encouraged you, offered clarity, and helped you feel seen in the places you needed it most. Now that you have finished the book, here are a few ways to keep moving forward with support and intention.

Access Your Free Resources

As a thank-you for reading, I have created a private space just for you. This page includes the tools referenced throughout the book. You can access it directly here:

www.wildernesswisdombook.com/resources

Inside, you will find:

The Glow Reset Meditation

A five-minute audio to help calm your body and nourish your soul. I recorded it in Hawaii during a season when I, too, needed a reset. I hope it brings you the peace and clarity it brought me.

The Compass Comeback Tool

A printable PDF for self-reflection and direction when you feel off track.

"True North" by Theresa Estel

A special song inspired by the message of this book and the journey to find your way.

A sneak peek at the 5-Day Compass Comeback Challenge
A guided experience to help you reset and begin again.

*This resource page is not searchable and is intended only for readers. Please do not share the link publicly.

Share A Review

If this book supported you in your healing or growth, I would be so grateful if you would leave a review. Your feedback helps other women find this work and begin their own journey through the wilderness.

How to Leave a Review:

- Go to the retailer where you purchased the book
- Click on "Write a Review"
- Share what encouraged or resonated with you

Your words matter and help this book reach those who may need it most.

Want More Support?

Learn more about **The Glow Forward Collective**, upcoming workshops, and coaching opportunities by visiting the main site:

www.thewildernesscompass.com

You are never as alone as you feel. Let this be the beginning of your comeback.

Always remember this: no matter how far down the pit you have fallen, your purpose is never out of reach. **You were made to rise.**

Love,

About The Author

Kris Cala is a life and business coach, speaker, and author who empowers women to reclaim their faith, power, and purpose after life has shaken their foundation. As the founder of The Wilderness Compass, she helps women move forward with clarity and confidence through seasons of change, loss, and transformation.

Through her coaching, workshops, and writing, Kris creates spaces where women stop feeling stuck and start rising, equipped with tools, community, and a renewed sense of direction for the life ahead.

www.ingramcontent.com/pod-product-compliance
Lightning Source LLC
Chambersburg PA
CBHW021623120626
46545CB00001B/365